THE SUCCESS IS WITHIN YOU
IT'S NOT ABOUT MONEY; IT'S ABOUT YOU...

Editora Appris Ltda.
1.ª Edição - Copyright© 2025 dos autores
Direitos de Edição Reservados à Editora Appris Ltda.

Nenhuma parte desta obra poderá ser utilizada indevidamente, sem estar de acordo com a Lei nº 9.610/98. Se incorreções forem encontradas, serão de exclusiva responsabilidade de seus organizadores. Foi realizado o Depósito Legal na Fundação Biblioteca Nacional, de acordo com as Leis n°s 10.994, de 14/12/2004, e 12.192, de 14/01/2010.

Catalogação na Fonte
Elaborado por: Dayanne Leal Souza
Bibliotecária CRB 9/2162

```
C794t      Cordeiro, Anderson Dornelas
2025         The success is within you: it's not about Money; it's about you... /
           Anderson Dornelas Cordeiro. – 1. ed. – Curitiba: Appris, 2025.
              159 p. ; 21 cm.


              ISBN 978-65-250-7569-3


              1. Self-development. 2. Motivation. 3. Overcoming. 4. Activation.
           I. Cordeiro, Anderson Dornelas. II. Título.

                                                         CDD – 155.7
```

Livro de acordo com a normalização técnica da ABNT

Appris
editorial

Editora e Livraria Appris Ltda.
Av. Manoel Ribas, 2265 – Mercês
Curitiba/PR – CEP: 80810-002
Tel. (41) 3156 - 4731
www.editoraappris.com.br

Printed in Brazil
Impresso no Brasil

Anderson Dornelas

THE SUCCESS IS WITHIN YOU
IT'S NOT ABOUT MONEY; IT'S ABOUT YOU...

Curitiba, PR
2025

FICHA TÉCNICA

EDITORIAL	Augusto V. de A. Coelho
	Sara C. de Andrade Coelho
COMITÊ EDITORIAL	Ana El Achkar (Universo/RJ)
	Andréa Barbosa Gouveia (UFPR)
	Jacques de Lima Ferreira (UNOESC)
	Marília Andrade Torales Campos (UFPR)
	Patrícia L. Torres (PUCPR)
	Roberta Ecleide Kelly (NEPE)
	Toni Reis (UP)
CONSULTORES	Luiz Carlos Oliveira
	Maria Tereza R. Pahl
	Marli C. de Andrade
SUPERVISORA EDITORIAL	Renata C. Lopes
PRODUÇÃO EDITORIAL	Maria Eduarda Pereira Paiz
REVISÃO	J. Vanderlei
DIAGRAMAÇÃO	Amélia Lopes
CAPA	Julie Lopes
	Renata Micelli
REVISÃO DE PROVA	Alice Ramos

I dedicate this book to Jesus Christ, my Lord and Savior. He is the source of my inspiration and the strength that guides me in all aspects of my life. I am deeply grateful for His unfathomable grace and sacrificial love. To Him be all the glory, now and forever.

SUMMARY

PRESENTATION 11

CHAPTER 1.
TURNING CHALLENGES INTO OPPORTUNITIES 13

CHAPTER 2.
USING THE MIND TO ACHIEVE SUCCESS 17

CHAPTER 3.
LEARNING FOR SUCCESS 23

CHAPTER 4.
FINANCIAL EDUCATION: THE KEY TO SUCCESS 33

CHAPTER 5.
PERSONAL CHANGE: THE PATH TO TRANSFORMATION 39

CHAPTER 6.
USING MIND AND EMOTIONS TO ACHIEVE
FINANCIAL FREEDOM 49

CHAPTER 7.
DEVELOPING FINANCIAL INTELLIGENCE 55

CHAPTER 8.
BALANCE AND FOCUS: LESSONS FROM THE GENIUSES
OF HISTORY 61

CHAPTER 9.
THE POWER OF SELF-DISCIPLINE ON THE JOURNEY
TO WEALTH 67

CHAPTER 10.
DEVELOPING THE WINNING MINDSET: THE POWER OF SELF-SUGGESTION AND BELIEF IN YOURSELF 81

CHAPTER 11.
EXPLORING THE CHARACTERISTICS OF SOME GREAT LEADERS 95

CHAPTER 12.
BECOMING THE MASTER OF YOURSELF: DISCIPLINE, ORGANIZATION, AND SELF-MASTERY TO ACHIEVE SUCCESS 99

CHAPTER 13.
LIFE AND WISDOM: PROCRASTINATION AND BRAVE BEGINNINGS.......................103

CHAPTER 14.
CHALLENGING LIMITS: THE ART OF RISKING AND THRIVING IN LIFE..107

CHAPTER 15.
MUHAMMAD: THE MIRACLE-LESS PROPHET AND HIS CONTROVERSIAL MESSAGE 113

CHAPTER 16.
THE POWER OF FAITH AND THE SUBCONSCIOUS..........................121

CHAPTER 17.
THE BRAIN AND CONSCIOUSNESS 123

CHAPTER 18.
DISCOVERING THE STRATEGIC ESSENCE: WHO WE ARE, WHERE WE COME FROM, AND WHERE WE'RE GOING............... 127

CHAPTER 19.
DIRECTING YOUR MIND TOWARDS GROWTH AND PROSPERITY 133

CHAPTER 20.
**AWAKENING YOUR INNER POTENTIAL:
THE KEY TO SUCCESS LIES WITHIN YOU!** 137

CHAPTER 21.
**AWAKENING TO CONSCIOUSNESS:
THE IMPORTANCE OF DEVELOPING OUR INNER ROOTS** 143

CHAPTER 22.
**THE LAW OF CAUSE AND EFFECT:
TRANSFORMING THE INTERIOR TO SHAPE THE EXTERIOR** 147

PRESENTATION

In a world obsessed with the pursuit of material wealth, we often forget how important it is to develop personal skills, cultivate a positive mindset, and adopt a balanced approach in all areas of life. As you delve into the pages of this book, you will discover the essential elements for achieving true and lasting success.

This book is not just about accumulating material wealth, but about developing a winning mindset that transcends the boundaries of financial prosperity. Here, you will find powerful tools and insights to strengthen your mindset, unlock your full potential, and build a solid foundation for success in all areas of your life.

We will explore the importance of cultivating healthy and authentic relationships. Genuine success is not achieved in isolation but through meaningful connections with others. We will learn to nurture positive relationships, build support networks, and collaborate with others towards common goals.

Finding purpose in our journey is another fundamental aspect discussed in this book. We will discover how to identify our values, passions, and unique talents, and align them with our goals and aspirations. By doing so, we can create a meaningful and fulfilling life, where every step we take is driven by a profound sense of purpose.

And, of course, we will address the importance of resilience in facing the obstacles that we will inevitably encounter on our journey towards success. We will learn to overcome challenges, deal with failure, and find inner strength to rise again, stronger and more determined than ever.

So, I invite you to embark on this journey of self-discovery and personal growth. This book is a practical and inspiring guide that will help you unlock the true potential within you and turn it into tangible achievements. Throughout the following pages, you will have the opportunity to explore concepts and strategies that will empower you to become the best version of yourself.

Remember that true success goes beyond surface appearances. It is about finding balance and harmony in all areas of life - whether in career, relationships, health, emotional well-being, or contribution to the world around you.

This book is an invitation for you to dive into a journey of self-transformation. Each chapter will offer valuable insights, inspiring examples, and practical tools to help you build a solid foundation for lasting success. Be ready to challenge your limiting beliefs, overcome fears, and embrace change. Success is in your hands, and it's time to harness the power within you.

Remember that success is not a final destination, but rather a continuous journey. This book will provide a "map" to guide you along the way, but it is up to you to take the necessary steps to achieve your goals and create the life you desire.

Embrace the opportunity to transform your life and discover true success. This is the moment to commit to your journey of personal growth and open yourself to the unlimited possibility within your reach. As you engage in this journey, you will witness the positive impact it will have on your own life and the lives of those around you.

Happy reading, and may this be just the beginning of your journey towards extraordinary success!

CHAPTER 1.

TURNING CHALLENGES INTO OPPORTUNITIES

A lean period can be tough for everyone, but it's important to remember that these extreme situations can help us grow and learn. When we face difficulties, we're forced to look at ourselves and reflect on our actions and motivations. We can discover what we're doing, why we're doing it, and what needs to change to achieve the best possible outcome. It's important to seize these opportunities to become better and more conscious individuals. When facing tough times, we may feel tempted to give up or be swept away by circumstances. However, it's crucial to remember that we have the power to choose how we react to situations. We can choose to succumb to despair, or we can choose to confront difficulties with courage and determination. By choosing to face difficulties, we can learn valuable lessons and grow as individuals. Remember that even in the toughest times, there's always something to learn and an opportunity to become better.

A wise person once said, "When a man is pushed, tormented, defeated... he has the opportunity to learn something." Difficulties are opportunities to grow and become a better person. With this new perspective, we should move forward, facing new challenges with courage and determination.

When facing discouragement, remember three crucial points:

1. Strategic Action: Discouragement often arises from self-pity and lack of action. To overcome it, it's essential to act strategically. Identify specific steps you can take to address the situation causing discouragement and start taking action. Action will bring a sense of progress and control, reducing the impact of discouragement.

2. Find Growth Opportunities: Even in the most discouraging situations, there's often a hidden opportunity for growth, maturity, and future success. Seek to identify what you can learn or how you can develop from the adverse experience. By finding purpose or a positive aspect in the situation, you can turn discouragement into motivation to grow and improve. "It's about making the best out of the worst."

3. Maintain Long-Term Perspective: Discouragement often makes us feel defeated and sees difficulties as insurmountable. However, it's important to remember that discouraging situations tend to diminish over time. Maintain a long-term perspective and remember that momentary setbacks don't define your future. Keep persisting toward your goals, knowing that difficulties are temporary and you can overcome them. Stay focused.

Chinese have a saying: "If you can endure a disaster for three years, it will become a blessing." In other words, failure is delay, not defeat. It's a temporary detour, not a dead end. Failure is something we can only avoid when we say, do, or are nothing. However, it's through these experiences of failure that we find the necessary opportunities and lessons to achieve success and personal growth. Knowing that the most famous and successful people of our time had to overcome obstacles as difficult as anyone can serve as motivation for us. It requires persistence and total commitment to our goals, but success is achievable.

An example of this is Thomas Edison. Edison's father called him "useless," and the school principal he studied under said he would never succeed at anything. However, Edison didn't give up. He continued to work hard and eventually became one of the greatest inventors in history. This story shows us that even when we face difficulties and challenges, we can overcome them with determination and perseverance. No matter what others say or think about us, we have the power to achieve our goals if we keep fighting for them.

Thomas Edison was an American inventor and entrepreneur known for being responsible for a series of inventions, including the incandescent light bulb. It is said that Thomas Edison owned over two thousand patents for inventions or important improvements in various devices. As a child, Edison lost his hearing at the age of 12. He worked as a salesman and telegraph operator. Later, he devoted himself to becoming an inventor. His first invention was a vote-counting machine, but it wasn't successful. Thomas Edison was married twice and had six children.

Henry Ford faced many difficulties during his high school years. He had a journey full of ups and downs, facing obstacles and challenges along the way. Despite these adversities, Ford never gave up his pursuit of knowledge and success. He persisted, overcame his limitations, and turned his experiences into valuable lessons that propelled him to become one of the greatest entrepreneurs and innovators of his time.

The machines of the world's greatest inventor, Leonardo da Vinci, a polymath born in Italy, one of the most important figures of the High Renaissance, who stood out as a scientist, mathematician, engineer, inventor, anatomist, painter, sculptor, architect, botanist, poet, and musician, conceived ideas far ahead of his time, such as a prototype of a helicopter, a tank, the use of solar energy, a calculator, among other inventions. He is thus considered one of the greatest geniuses in history. At the time, they were not given importance, and many would not have worked if they had not been put into practice.

Edwin Land, the inventor of the Polaroid Land camera, faced many challenges in trying to develop instant films. He described his efforts as an attempt to use impossible chemistry with nonexistent technology to create a product that could not be manufactured and for which there was no significant demand. However, instead of giving up, Land saw these obstacles as the perfect conditions for the creative mind.

This story shows us that even when we face seemingly insurmountable challenges, we can use our creativity and determination to find solutions. Obstacles can force us to think outside the box and find new ways to solve problems. Instead of discouraging us, challenges can motivate us to work even harder and achieve our goals.

Edwin Land's story shows us that even when we face seemingly insurmountable challenges, we can overcome them with creativity and determination. Instead of giving up, we can use our creative mind to find solutions and overcome obstacles.

Another example of someone who overcame challenges to achieve success is Steve Jobs. Jobs was fired from Apple, the company he co-founded, but he didn't give up. He continued working on his projects and eventually returned to Apple and helped transform it into one of the most successful companies in the world.

Jobs' story shows us that even when we face rejections and failures, we can keep fighting for our dreams. With determination and perseverance, we can overcome obstacles and achieve success.

"Eat the bitter to taste the sweet" is a saying that conveys profound wisdom. This phrase reminds us that when we experience painful experiences, we have the opportunity to strengthen ourselves. True transformation depends on our ability to find something beyond the pain.

When we face difficult times, it's natural to feel sadness, frustration, and even despair. However, if we can look beyond the surface of pain, we can find valuable lessons and opportunities for personal growth.

When facing adversity, we can develop resilience by learning to adapt and overcome obstacles. We can discover an inner strength we didn't know we had. We can gain wisdom and understanding about ourselves and the world around us.

Therefore, when life offers us bitterness, we should remember that it's just part of the process. By facing it head-on and seeking the meaning behind it, we'll discover that the sweet taste of overcoming and growth is even more rewarding. Transformation is within our reach, as long as we have the courage to face.

CHAPTER 2.

USING THE MIND TO ACHIEVE SUCCESS

The human mind is a powerful tool that sets us apart from other creatures on Earth. Everything that is important to us, such as love for family, our beliefs, talents, knowledge, and skills, is reflected by the mind. It is through the use of our mind that we can achieve our goals and fulfill our dreams.

Often, the mind is the last place we turn to for help when facing a problem. Why does this happen? Why don't we automatically turn to our vast mental resources when facing challenges? The answer is simple: many people have never learned to think effectively. Instead of facing their problems head-on, they prefer distractions, escapes, and quick fixes.

However, true success lies within ourselves. By learning to use our mind effectively, we can face our challenges with confidence and determination. We can develop our critical thinking and problem-solving skills and use our mind to find creative and innovative solutions to the challenges we face. Remember that success is within you, and you have the power to achieve it through the effective use of your mind. To develop our thinking skills and use our mind effectively, we can start by practicing reflection and introspection. We can take time to think about our goals, challenges, and dreams and try to find creative solutions to the problems we face. We can also practice meditation or other relaxation techniques to calm our mind and focus on our thoughts.

Additionally, we can develop our critical thinking skills by exposing ourselves to new ideas and perspectives. We can read books, attend lectures, or engage in discussions that challenge us to think differently and expand our horizons. By doing so, we can develop our ability to analyze information, evaluate arguments, and make informed decisions.

Remember that success is within you, and you have the power to achieve it through the effective use of your mind. By developing your thinking skills and using your mind effectively, you can face your challenges with confidence and determination and achieve your goals.

Planning for success is a crucial step in the journey to achieve our goals. By carefully planning our actions and strategies, we can increase our chances of success and avoid obstacles and setbacks.

To effectively plan for success, we can start by clearly defining our goals and setting realistic targets. It is important to be specific and detailed when defining our goals so that we can measure our progress and adjust our strategies as needed.

It is also important to identify the resources and tools we will need to achieve our goals. This may include skills, knowledge, time, money, and support from others. Remember that planning is an ongoing process and that we must be willing to adjust our strategies as needed. With careful and effective planning, we can increase our chances of success and achieve our goals.

At the heart of the journey to success, there is a fundamental element that is often overlooked: self-awareness. It is the ability to look within ourselves, explore the depths of the mind, and understand who we really are. Self-awareness is a journey of self-discovery that allows us to understand our strengths, weaknesses, passions, and deepest values.

In a busy world full of distractions, many people live their lives without ever stopping to reflect on who they really are. They follow the paths laid out by society, the expectations of others, and external pressures without ever questioning whether these choices align with their values and personal purposes.

However, when we know ourselves deeply, we can set clear goals and make decisions aligned with our essence. Self-awareness allows us to identify our unique talents and abilities and helps us make the most of these qualities. When we are aware of our weaknesses, we can work on them and seek opportunities for personal growth.

By knowing our passions, we can direct our energy towards what truly inspires and motivates us. When we align our goals with our deepest values, we find a sense of purpose and meaning in everything we do. Self-awareness allows us to live an authentic life, in harmony with our true convictions.

Imagine yourself in a boat sailing the ocean without a clear destination. Without knowing your navigation skills, your resources, and your goals, you would be at the mercy of the currents and tides, without a defined direction. Now, imagine yourself in that same boat, but with a detailed map, a reliable compass, and knowledge of your navigation skills. You would be prepared to face any challenges that arise.

Self-awareness is like a map for our personal journey. It helps us understand where we are, where we want to go, and how we can get there. When we know ourselves deeply, we can make conscious and intentional decisions that lead us towards our goals.

Throughout life, we face many challenges and obstacles. Self-awareness helps us face them with confidence and resilience. When we know our strengths, we can use them to overcome difficulties. When we are aware of our weaknesses, we can seek support and resources to overcome them.

Self-awareness also helps us build healthy and meaningful relationships. When we understand our emotional needs, we can communicate them clearly and assertively. When we know our limits, we can establish healthy boundaries in our relationships. When we are in tune with our values, we can build relationships based on mutual respect and trust. It allows us to live a full and authentic life. It helps us define our goals, make decisions aligned with our values, and face life's challenges with confidence and resilience. By embarking on this journey of self-discovery, we open the doors to a world of unlimited possibilities.

The mind is a fertile field where our thoughts and beliefs flourish. Our perspective shapes the way we see the world and determines our attitude towards the challenges we face. That's why cultivating a positive and optimistic mindset is so important for our success and well-being.

A positive mindset doesn't mean ignoring problems or denying the existence of difficulties. On the contrary, it's a conscious choice to see beyond adversities and find the positive potential in every situation. It's the ability to direct our thoughts towards what is constructive, inspiring, and motivating.

When we adopt a positive mindset, we can turn challenges into opportunities for growth. Instead of feeling defeated by difficulties, we see each obstacle as a chance to learn, evolve, and become stronger. This perspective drives us to seek creative solutions and persevere in the face of adversity.

Moreover, positive thinking has a profound impact on our motivation. When we believe that we are capable of overcoming challenges and achieving our goals, we find the energy and determination necessary to move forward. Positive mindset nurtures a growth mindset, where we see failures as learning opportunities and believe in our unlimited potential.

Resilience is also a fruit of a positive mindset. Faced with life's storms, we are able to adapt, recover, and move forward with courage and hope. Instead of being discouraged by setbacks, we find inner strength to face setbacks and build a full and meaningful life.

By cultivating a positive mindset, we can transform our reality and positively influence the people around us.

Cultivating a positive mindset is a continuous process that requires practice and dedication. Here are some tips to help you develop a more positive perspective:

Practice gratitude: Take time every day to reflect on the things you are grateful for. This can include people, experiences, opportunities, and even small moments of joy. Gratitude helps us focus on the positive in our lives and cultivate an attitude of appreciation.

Challenge negative thoughts: When negative thoughts arise, challenge them with questions like "Is this really true?" or "Is there another way to see this situation?". This helps us question our limiting beliefs and develop a more balanced perspective.

CHAPTER 3.

LEARNING FOR SUCCESS

"The cure for our ignorance is our willingness to learn."

The desire to learn is a powerful engine that drives our personal growth and empowers us to overcome challenges.

Through the willingness to learn, we broaden our horizons and expand our understanding of the world. It encourages us to explore new topics, acquire new skills, and deepen our understanding in areas that interest us. Curiosity becomes our ally, propelling us to ask questions, seek answers, and unravel the mysteries that surround us.

Moreover, it helps us adapt in a constantly changing world. It makes us flexible and open to new ideas, allowing us to adjust to the transformations that occur in our lives and in society as a whole. By embracing continuous learning, we are prepared to face challenges and seize the opportunities that arise.

The willingness to learn also makes us more humble. We acknowledge that we don't know everything and are willing to listen to different perspectives. By setting aside our own intellectual arrogance, we open ourselves to the wisdom of others and are more willing to consider new ideas and viewpoints. This enriches us and makes us more complete individuals.

Therefore, the cure for ignorance lies in our willingness to learn. It is a constant commitment to expanding our knowledge, developing our skills, and seeking the truth. By embracing this willingness to learn, we are opening the doors to a world of discovery and personal growth.

"Success is the progressive realization of a worthy goal."

When we set meaningful goals and work diligently to achieve them, we experience a sense of progress and accomplishment that propels us forward.

The key to success lies in setting goals that align with our values, passions, and abilities. By choosing goals that are meaningful to us, we increase our motivation and commitment to the process of achieving them. These worthy goals may vary from person to person—it could be a rewarding career, building a loving family, contributing to society, or pursuing excellence in a specific skill.

However, success is not just the end result. It is a continuous journey of learning, growth, and self-development. As we progress towards our goals, we face challenges and obstacles, but we also acquire new skills, expand our knowledge, and develop resilience.

Success is not limited to external achievements such as wealth or recognition. It also includes feelings of personal satisfaction, self-acceptance, and happiness. It is finding a healthy balance between our personal and professional lives, taking care of our health and well-being, nurturing meaningful relationships, and finding purpose and meaning in our actions.

It's important to remember that success is relative and unique to each individual. What may be considered success for one person may not be the same for another. It is crucial to define our own parameters of success and not constantly compare ourselves to others. Everyone has their own journey and their own pace.

In summary, success is the combination of setting worthy goals that align with our values and passions, progressing towards those goals with dedication and commitment, and finding satisfaction and fulfillment along the way. It is a personal journey of continuous growth and self-development, where we learn from our mistakes, adapt to ever-changing circumstances, and seek constant improvement.

Furthermore, success is not a final destination but a continuous process. As we achieve goals and objectives, it's important to set new challenges and continue evolving. Success is rooted in the constant pursuit of improvement and the desire to grow and expand our horizons.

However, it's essential to remember that success is not guaranteed and may require effort, perseverance, and dedication. There may be setbacks along the way and moments when we face challenges and obstacles. However, it is in these situations that we have the opportunity to learn, grow, and become stronger.

Success is intrinsically linked to happiness and personal fulfillment. Balancing professional, personal, and emotional success is important, and seeking a purposeful life is fundamental. Each person defines success uniquely, following their values and personal aspirations.

Success is an individual and personal journey. It is the constant pursuit of worthy goals, personal and professional growth, and lasting happiness. It is continuously progressing towards meaningful objectives, valuing not only the results but also the journey itself.

Anyone striving to achieve a goal is successful.

Success should not only be measured by final results but also by perseverance, learning, and growth along the way. Every obstacle overcome, every lesson learned, and every experience lived are elements that contribute to personal success.

It's important to remember that success is relative and unique to each individual. What may be considered success for one person may not have the same meaning for another. It is crucial not to compare ourselves to others but to focus on our own goals and personal progress.

Furthermore, success is not a final destination but an ever-evolving journey. As we reach one goal, new challenges arise, propelling us to continue growing and reaching new heights.

Therefore, whatever your goal may be, remember that true success lies in the journey you undertake, in the positive impact you have on others' lives, and in the happiness and satisfaction you find in following your values and passions.

Success is not in achieving a goal, although that is what is often considered success by society. In fact, success lies in the journey toward that goal. We are successful when we work to achieve something we desire in our lives. It is in this process that the best of ourselves emerges.

Isaac Newton expressed this idea when he wrote about the law of inertia, which states that an object in motion tends to stay in motion. Similarly, Miguel de Cervantes wanted to convey this message when he wrote: "The road is better than the inn." That is, we are better when we are in the process of advancing, thinking, planning, and working towards something we want to accomplish.

Winning is not something that occurs sporadically. It is something that should happen continuously. It's not about doing things right only occasionally. It's about doing things right all the time. Success is not an isolated event but a continuous commitment to excellence and the relentless pursuit of our goals.

There is no endpoint to success because it is a continuous process. As we achieve one goal, new challenges arise, and new goals are set. It's important to recognize that success is not only measured by external results or material achievements but also by our journey of self-development, learning, and personal growth.

True success goes beyond what is perceived externally. It is rooted in how we face challenges, overcome obstacles, and become better people along the way. Success lies in cultivating a growth mindset, constantly seeking improvement, and finding satisfaction in the gradual progression towards our goals.

In this process, it's essential to remember that success is highly individual and subjective. Each person has their own aspirations, values, and definitions of success. It is essential to avoid comparisons with others and focus on our own path.

Therefore, success lies in the journey towards our goals, in the commitment to do our best, in learning from failures, and in never ceasing to pursue personal growth. It's a mindset, a way of life, where we embrace the journey and find satisfaction not only in the final destination but in every step along the way.

Throughout the journey, it's essential to maintain focus and determination. Setting clear and achievable goals can help keep track and motivation. Additionally, it's important to cultivate a mindset of continuous learning, be open to new ideas and perspectives, and seek opportunities for growth and development.

It's also valuable to surround yourself with people who support and encourage your success. Having a support network, such as mentors, friends, and colleagues, can provide emotional support and inspiration during challenging times. Collaboration and knowledge sharing with others can also generate new ideas and enriching perspectives.

When striving for success, it's important to take care of yourself. This includes maintaining a healthy balance between work, personal life, rest, and self-care. Long-lasting success is built on a solid foundation of physical and mental well-being.

Remember that success is not a final destination but a continuous process. Celebrate your achievements along the way, no matter how small, and recognize that each step is an important part of your journey. Stay focused, perseverant, and committed to your personal growth, and keep learning and evolving along your path to success.

"Seven things you should do every day:

These seven actions have the potential to contribute to a balanced and successful life.

1. Setting clear and achievable goals means establishing specific and realistic objectives that are possible to achieve. It's

important that these goals are well defined, so you know exactly what you want to achieve and can measure your progress over time.

By setting clear goals, you create direction and purpose for your daily actions. This allows you to focus on activities that truly contribute to achieving those goals, avoiding dispersion and wasting time and energy.

Moreover, it's crucial that goals are achievable. This means they should be realistic and feasible within the context you are in. By setting goals that are achievable, you increase your motivation and confidence, as you see that you are making progress and getting tangible results.

Setting clear and achievable goals is an important step towards a balanced and successful life, as it provides focus, direction, and a sense of purpose. This allows you to organize yourself, plan your actions, and work consistently towards what you want to achieve. Increase your energy and promote social connections.

2. Thinking: By setting aside daily time to think, we can cultivate mental clarity, stimulate creativity, and enhance our problem-solving skills. It is through thinking that we are able to organize our ideas, analyze different perspectives, and make more informed decisions.

By thinking regularly, we are able to set meaningful goals for ourselves, establish clear priorities, and plan our actions more effectively. Thinking helps us identify opportunities, anticipate possible obstacles, and devise strategies to achieve success in various areas of our lives.

Therefore, dedicating time to think is not a luxury but an essential practice for personal and professional growth. By allowing ourselves this space for reflection, we can reap the benefits of a clearer mind, stimulated creativity, and an enhanced ability to solve problems intelligently.

3. Dancing: That's right, dancing is a form of art and a pleasurable physical activity. By dancing regularly, you can improve your physical fitness, increase flexibility, coordination, and release mood-enhancing endorphins. Dance is also a way to express emotions, relieve stress, and connect with others through movement.

Therefore, set aside time to dance regularly. It can be in a dance class, in your living room, or even listening to your favorite music while moving. Let yourself be carried away by the music, feel the rhythm, and allow your body to surrender to expression. Dance is a wonderful way to have fun, express yourself, and improve your overall well-being.

Balance is key. Find time to laugh, exercise your mind and dance, and enjoy the benefits each of these activities brings to your life. Harness the power of laughter, positive thinking, and dance to improve your day, promote happiness, and seek success in everything you do.

4. Learning: Continuous learning is fundamental for personal and professional growth. It's important to set aside time every day to acquire knowledge and expand horizons. There are various ways to engage in constant study.

One way is to explore new topics and areas of interest. Be open to learning about different subjects, even if they are not directly related to your field of work. This can bring new perspectives and insights that can be applied in various areas of your life.

Continuous learning provides many benefits. It expands your perspective, enhances your skills, and enables you to face challenges confidently. Moreover, it demonstrates a commitment to personal and professional development, which can open doors to future opportunities.

Therefore, dedicate time daily to study, regardless of the chosen area. The pursuit of knowledge is a continuous and rewarding journey that contributes to your growth and success in all aspects of life.

5. Connecting: Connecting with other people is essential for success and well-being in various aspects of life. It's important to set aside time to connect with true friends, family, and colleagues.

By cultivating meaningful relationships, you can share experiences, seek emotional support, and offer support to others. Connecting with others nurtures the spirit, provides a sense of belonging, and strengthens the support network on your journey towards success.

Allocate time to build solid relationships, based on trust, respect, and empathy. Listen actively and show genuine interest in others. Share your own experiences, ideas, and emotions openly and authentically.

In addition to personal interactions, also use virtual means to maintain connections. Social networks, messaging apps, and video calls can be great tools to connect with people who are geographically distant.

It's important to remember that the quality of connections is more important than quantity. Prioritize investing time and energy in true and meaningful relationships, rather than seeking a vast network of superficial contacts.

By connecting with others, you strengthen interpersonal bonds, receive emotional support, and also have the opportunity to offer your support to others. This mutual exchange of support and care is essential for individual growth and for building a support community that accompanies you on your journey towards success.

Therefore, allocate time and effort to cultivate meaningful connections with those around you, both personally and virtually. This practice nurtures your soul, strengthens your sense of belonging, and contributes to a solid support network on your path to success.

6. Setting goals: Setting clear and achievable goals is essential to direct efforts and measure progress in various areas of life. Daily,

it's important to set realistic and specific goals that drive personal growth. It's essential to consider different aspects of life, such as career, health, relationships, and personal development. This allows for a holistic approach to self-development and achieving success in various spheres.

When setting goals, it's advisable to make them SMART: specific, measurable, achievable, relevant, and time-bound. This provides clarity and direction to your path. For example, instead of simply saying "I want to improve my health," a SMART goal would be "to exercise for 30 minutes, five times a week, for the next three months."

By consistently working towards established goals, you create a sense of purpose and motivation. This happens because you can see the progress you are making and feel fulfilled as you reach each step. Additionally, goal-setting helps focus energy and resources effectively, avoiding distractions and unnecessary activities.

Remember to periodically adjust your goals, if necessary, to ensure they remain relevant and aligned with your long-term objectives. Celebrating achievements upon reaching goals is also important to maintain motivation and enthusiasm along the way.

Therefore, setting realistic and specific goals, and consistently working to achieve them, is an effective strategy to create a sense of purpose, motivation, and direction in your life.

7. Practicing gratitude and self-care: Practicing gratitude and self-care are two important practices to promote emotional and mental well-being.

Gratitude involves directing our attention to the positive things in our lives and cultivating a sense of appreciation and recognition for them. By practicing gratitude, we develop a positive mindset and focus on the good things around us, even in challenging situations. This helps us find happiness and satisfaction in the present, strengthens our relationships, and improves our overall perspective on life.

Self-care refers to taking deliberate steps to take care of ourselves, both physically and emotionally. This involves prioritizing our health and well-being, setting aside time for activities that rejuvenate us and bring us joy. Self-care can include regular physical exercise, healthy eating, adequate rest, relaxation practices, hobbies, and seeking emotional support when needed. By practicing self-care, we are investing in our own health and happiness, which empowers us to better cope with stress, prevent burnout, and maintain a healthy balance in our lives.

Both gratitude and self-care are practices that require intentionality and consistency. By incorporating them into our daily routine, we can experience significant benefits, such as increased happiness, emotional resilience, more positive relationships, and a greater ability to cope with challenges that arise. Therefore, cultivating gratitude and dedicating time to self-care are valuable investments in our overall health and well-being. Remember that success is an individual journey.

CHAPTER 4.

FINANCIAL EDUCATION: THE KEY TO SUCCESS

Let's discuss money and its importance. It is essential to learn about finances, but unfortunately, this subject is not addressed in schools. Educational institutions focus on academic and professional skills, but neglect financial education. This may explain why many successful professionals, such as doctors, bank managers, and accountants, face financial problems throughout their lives. Even educated politicians and public officials make financial decisions without the necessary knowledge in the field, contributing to national debt.

Therefore, it is essential to seek knowledge about personal finances to achieve financial success. It is important to learn about budgeting, saving, investments, and financial planning. There are several ways to acquire these skills, such as reading books, taking courses, or seeking financial advice. By empowering yourself in this area, you can make more informed financial decisions and achieve financial stability.

Furthermore, it is important to remember that money is just a tool to achieve our goals and fulfill our dreams. It is important to manage it wisely and responsibly, but it is also important not to let it dominate our lives. By acquiring financial skills and making informed decisions, we can use money to improve our lives and achieve our goals without letting it control us.

A fundamental aspect of financial success is establishing a budget and a financial plan. This involves setting financial goals, tracking expenses, saving for the future, and avoiding excessive debt. By creating a realistic budget and keeping track of your finances, you can develop a solid foundation for a healthy and prosperous financial life.

A smart approach to money involves making it work for you. This includes learning about different forms of investment, such as stocks, real estate, mutual funds, etc. By investing appropriately and diversifying, you can increase your net worth over time and enjoy the benefits of financial growth.

In addition to the practical and technical aspects of money, it is important to cultivate a prosperous mindset. This involves believing that you deserve prosperity, eliminating limiting beliefs about money, and adopting a positive attitude towards abundance. By developing a prosperous mindset, you will be able to attract financial opportunities and make decisions that promote financial growth and success.

Remember that each person has a unique relationship with money and that financial strategies may vary according to individual circumstances. It is important to seek knowledge, adapt information to your needs, and make financial decisions based on your goals and personal values.

Excessive indebtedness can be an obstacle to financial success. It is essential to develop debt management skills, such as prioritizing payments, negotiating lower interest rates, and creating a plan to gradually pay off debts. By effectively dealing with debts, you can regain financial control and create space to build a solid foundation for the future.

Having an emergency fund is a fundamental part of a healthy financial life. Set aside a portion of your income regularly for savings that can be accessed in case of emergencies, such as medical expenses, home repairs, or job loss. Having an emergency fund provides security and financial peace of mind, allowing you to deal with challenges without compromising your progress.

Financial success goes beyond accumulating personal wealth and includes the ability to contribute to causes you value and help those in less fortunate situations. By sharing your prosperity with others, you not only create a positive impact on their lives but also cultivate a mindset of abundance and gratitude.

Financial generosity is a powerful way to give back to society and make a difference. This can involve donations to non-profit organizations, support for community projects, contributions to education programs, or even helping individuals in direct need. By directing your financial resources to meaningful causes, you become a change agent and promote a better world.

In addition to the positive impact you provide to others, practicing financial generosity also brings personal benefits. Cultivating an abundance mindset means recognizing that you have resources to share and appreciating the opportunity to make a difference. This mindset creates a sense of gratitude for your own prosperity and a greater sense of purpose in life.

By sharing your prosperity, you establish a virtuous cycle where the benefits extend beyond the financial aspect. Generosity creates deeper connections with those around you, strengthens relationships, and builds a supportive community. It also inspires others to follow suit and practice generosity in their own lives.

Therefore, as you pursue financial success, remember the importance of contributing to causes you value and helping others. Be a change agent and leave your positive mark on the world. Financial generosity not only benefits those who receive your help but also enriches your own life and promotes a more harmonious and inclusive society.

"In the Bible, we find valuable teachings about the importance of contribution and the blessings that accompany this generous act. In 2 Corinthians 9:6, we read: 'The one who sows sparingly will also reap sparingly, and the one who sows bountifully will also reap bountifully.' This passage reminds us that when we share our resources generously, we are planting seeds that have the potential to bring us an abundant harvest.

Furthermore, Proverbs 11:25 teaches us: 'A generous person will prosper; whoever refreshes others will be refreshed.' These words remind us that generosity not only blesses those who receive but also brings blessings and prosperity to those who give. When we are willing to help others, whether with our time, talent, or financial resources, we are graced with a sense of purpose and inner joy.

It is important to note that contribution is not limited to financial resources alone. In Matthew 25:40, Jesus teaches that helping the needy is akin to helping Him directly: 'Truly I tell you, whatever you did for one of the least of these brothers and sisters of mine, you did for me.' This shows us that any act of kindness and generosity, regardless of its magnitude, is valuable and rewarded.

Therefore, may we be inspired by these biblical words and seek opportunities to contribute to the well-being of others. Let us be generous in our actions, sharing our resources and talents with those in need. In doing so, we pave the way for blessings and prosperity to flow into our lives, and we live according to divine principles of love, compassion, and service to others.

Remember that contribution should not be motivated by greed or the pursuit of selfish rewards, but by a generous heart and a sincere desire to make a difference in the lives of others. In 2 Corinthians 9:7, the Bible reminds us: 'Each of you should give what you have decided in your heart to give, not reluctantly or under compulsion, for God loves a cheerful giver.' It is important that our giving be a reflection of our gratitude to God and our desire to share His blessings with the needy.

Furthermore, the Bible teaches us to be faithful stewards of the resources that God has entrusted to us. In Luke 12:48, Jesus says: 'From everyone who has been given much, much will be demanded; and from the one who has been entrusted with much, much more will be asked.' This reminds us that if we have been blessed with abundance, we have a responsibility to use our resources wisely and generously, contributing to the well-being of others. In doing so, we demonstrate our trust in God as our provider and acknowledge our role as agents of His goodness and love in the world.

Therefore, may we reflect on these biblical teachings and seek ways to contribute to the improvement of others' lives. Whether through financial donations to righteous causes, offering practical help to those in need, or sharing our talents and abilities, each act of generosity has the potential to make a significant difference. By living according to these principles, we open space for the manifestation of God's blessings in our own lives and in the lives of those around us.

The path to financial success is an ongoing journey. It is important to regularly review your financial strategies, reassess your goals, and make adjustments as necessary. As your circumstances and priorities change over time, you can adapt your strategies to reflect your new goals and needs.

Remember that money is a powerful tool when used wisely and responsibly. Always seek to balance your financial goals with a happy and fulfilling life, remembering that money is not the sole indicator of success and happiness. While it is important to seek financial stability, it is equally crucial to cultivate meaningful relationships, take care of physical and mental health, pursue personal growth, and find purpose in your life.

True financial success goes beyond accumulating material wealth. It is about finding a healthy balance between pursuing financial prosperity and seeking a fulfilling and meaningful life.

By adopting a conscious and balanced approach to money, you can create a solid foundation for financial success and a satisfying life. Remember that financial skills can be learned and improved over time, and that every step you take towards a financially healthy life is a step towards your personal success.

Keep exploring, learning, and growing on your financial journey, always remembering to adapt to your individual circumstances and seek balance between material prosperity and inner happiness.

CHAPTER 5.

PERSONAL CHANGE: THE PATH TO TRANSFORMATION

"There is a distinction between being temporarily financially disadvantaged and being permanently poor. The condition of being broke is transient, while the condition of being poor is enduring."

Most people want everyone in the world to change, except themselves. But I tell you: it is easier to change yourself than everyone else. In addition to understanding the importance of contribution and the blessings it brings, it is essential to recognize that it is easier to change oneself than to try to change everyone else around us. Personal change requires self-reflection, self-awareness, and a sincere commitment to continuous growth and development.

The Bible encourages us to seek inner transformation in Romans 12:2, where it is written: "Do not conform to the pattern of this world, but be transformed by the renewing of your mind." This passage reminds us that true change begins in the mind and heart. It is necessary to abandon old patterns of thinking and behavior that limit us and adopt a renewed mindset aligned with divine principles and values.

By growing and perfecting ourselves individually, we can serve as an example and inspiration to others. Our actions speak louder than our words. When we live according to biblical teachings, we demonstrate the transformative power of love, kindness, and compassion. This can positively influence those around us and gradually inspire genuine change in their lives.

However, we must keep in mind that personal change does not mean that we should ignore or give up helping others. On the contrary, as we transform ourselves, we become more capable of offering support and encouragement to those around us. We can share our experiences, knowledge, and wisdom, encouraging others to follow a path of growth and self-transformation.

By embracing the notion that it is easier to change oneself than everyone else, we develop a humble and realistic stance. We recognize that each individual has their own free will and growth timeline. Therefore, instead of trying to impose changes on others, we focus on our own improvement and allow our light to shine as a beacon of hope and inspiration. This not only brings us inner peace but also empowers us to play a significant role in transforming the world around us.

So let us continue to seek change within ourselves, strengthening our connection with God, cultivating virtues such as love, patience, kindness, and humility, and constantly striving to grow spiritually. By doing so, we become agents of positive change, capable of impacting not only our own lives but also the lives of those around us.

Always remember that, while it is easier to change oneself than everyone else, our personal transformation can be a powerful and inspiring influence on others. Therefore, let us continue to strive for excellence in our own paths, illuminating the world with our values and actions, and trusting that, through our dedication to growth and service, we can make a lasting difference in the lives of those with whom we share this journey.

May the pursuit of personal change and love for others be the foundation of our lives, guiding us toward a full and meaningful existence. And may we, together, build a better world, one heart at a time.

When facing fear, it is essential to remember that financial security does not need to be achieved solely through conventional employment. There are many opportunities to explore entrepreneurship, investments, and other forms of income generation. By adopting a mindset of courage and resilience, it is possible to overcome fears related to finances and pursue paths that provide greater personal fulfillment and financial freedom.

It is important to recognize that fear is a natural emotion, but we should not allow it to paralyze us. Instead, we should use it as a motivation to challenge ourselves and seek new possibilities. Often, it is outside of our comfort zone that we find the best opportunities for growth and success.

When facing financial fear, it is helpful to seek knowledge and education about financial management, investments, and entrepreneurship. The more we understand how money works and the opportunities for financial growth, the more empowered we will be to make informed decisions and reduce associated risks.

Furthermore, it is important to create a solid financial plan, setting clear goals and developing healthy financial habits. This includes saving, investing wisely, and building a financial safety net to deal with unexpected expenses.

Facing financial fear requires courage, determination, and perseverance. It is a continuous process, but the results can be transformative. By overcoming fears related to finances, we make room for a fuller and more fulfilled life, where we can pursue our true dreams and goals. Therefore, do not let fear dominate you, face it head-on, and build a financially satisfying and meaningful life.

When facing financial fear, it is also important to develop a mindset of abundance and confidence. Instead of focusing on the fear of scarcity, direct your energy towards believing in your abilities, capacities, and the existence of opportunities around you.

An effective way to deal with fear is to seek support and guidance. Look for mentors, financial coaches, or successful people in the field you wish to venture into. Learn from their experiences and let them inspire and guide you along the way.

Furthermore, be willing to take calculated risks. Fear often arises from uncertainty and the possibility of failure. However, remember that failure is part of the process of learning and growth. Be flexible and adaptable, willing to adjust your approach and learn from challenges rather than letting fear paralyze you.

When facing financial fear, it is also important to have a contingency plan. Be prepared to deal with possible setbacks and unexpected events along the way. This may include creating financial reserves, establishing an emergency fund, and exploring alternative options if your initial attempts do not work out as expected.

Remember that facing financial fear is a gradual process. Celebrate small victories along the way, celebrate your progress, and be patient with yourself. Believe in your potential and your ability to overcome the obstacles that arise.

In summary, facing financial fear requires a combination of courage, knowledge, strategic planning, and perseverance. By adopting a mindset of abundance, seeking support, and taking concrete actions, you are on the path to overcoming fear and achieving a more prosperous and fulfilling financial life.

The truth is that the beginning can be scary. There are uncertainties, risks, and the possibility of facing unexpected challenges. However, it is also an opportunity to grow, learn, and discover new horizons. By embracing change and starting anew, we open ourselves to infinite possibilities and personal growth.

It is important to remember that financial success is not only measured by the balance in our bank account. It is about finding a balance between earning a living and finding personal fulfillment. It may be necessary to adjust our standards of living, adopt an entrepreneurial mindset, and be open to seeking different sources of income. Sometimes, this may involve taking calculated risks, but it is through these experiences that we can expand our horizons and find true purpose in our work.

Therefore, for those who are stuck in jobs that do not bring them satisfaction, it is important to question the fear that keeps them there. Is it the fear of not being able to pay the bills that is paralyzing their pursuit of a more meaningful life? If so, it is necessary to explore options that may offer greater fulfillment and personal satisfaction. This may involve seeking new career opportunities, considering starting your own business, or even pursuing freelance work or side projects that can provide a greater sense of purpose.

It is important to remember that overcoming fear does not happen overnight. It requires courage, determination, and a well-structured plan. It is necessary to carefully assess financial circumstances, create an emergency reserve, and develop relevant skills for new areas of interest.

Furthermore, emotional support and encouragement from those around us can be invaluable in this process. Sharing our fears and aspirations with trusted friends, family, or mentors can provide a different perspective, helpful advice, and the support needed to take the first steps.

Remember that life is too short and valuable to be lived in constant fear and dissatisfaction. People have found success and happiness by following their dreams, even in the face of fear. It is important to remember that failure is part of the process of learning and growth, and that each obstacle is an opportunity to strengthen and move forward.

Therefore, have the courage to face fear, do not let it keep you trapped in a situation that does not bring you fulfillment. Be willing to start anew, explore new paths, and seek a life that is aligned with your values and passions. Ultimately, it is your own well-being and happiness that are at stake, and they are worth fighting for. So challenge yourself to face the fear of not being able to pay the bills, turning it into motivation to seek creative and alternative solutions. Create a realistic financial plan, analyze your expenses, and identify areas for cuts or adjustments that can be made. Also, consider seeking professional help, such as financial consultants, for specialized guidance.

Furthermore, remember that fear is a normal emotion and we all face it at some point in our lives. It is important not to let it paralyze your actions or prevent you from reaching your true potential. Cultivate a mindset of confidence and self-esteem, remembering your abilities, talents, and past achievements. This will give you the necessary courage to move forward, even in the face of challenges.

Find sources of inspiration and success stories from people who have overcome fear and found fulfillment in their professional lives. This can help expand your vision and show that it is possible to achieve a balance between financial support and happiness at work.

Finally, remember that the process of overcoming fear and seeking a more satisfying professional life may take time. Be patient with yourself and celebrate each small victory along the way. The important thing is to take the first step and keep moving forward, even if it is towards an uncertain future.

Do not let the fear of not being able to pay the bills be the only reason keeping you trapped in an unhappy job. Be willing to explore your passions, discover your talents, and seek work that brings you true fulfillment. Remember that you deserve a professional life that makes you excited to wake up every morning. Therefore, have courage, trust yourself, and pursue your dreams. Continue to educate yourself and acquire new skills relevant to the current job market. Invest in courses, training, and continuous professional development. This can help increase your chances of finding a job you enjoy and that pays well.

Also, consider exploring different sectors or areas of work. Sometimes, finding a satisfying career requires exploring less conventional paths. Be open to new opportunities and do not be afraid to change direction if you feel it is the right path for you.

Furthermore, build a network of professional contacts. Networking can play a key role in job search and career advancement. Attend industry events, make connections through social media, and be willing to introduce yourself and share your professional goals with others. Sometimes, opportunities arise through connections and recommendations.

Do not be afraid to seek support and guidance in your professional journey. Look for mentors or coaches who can help you navigate challenges and advise on your career path. They can offer valuable insights, share experiences, and provide practical advice to help you achieve your goals.

Finally, maintain a positive and persistent attitude. The pursuit of a satisfying career can be challenging, but it is important not to give up. Believe in yourself, stay motivated, and keep moving forward, even when facing obstacles. With determination and perseverance, you can overcome fear and find a career that brings balance, satisfaction, and personal success.

Remember that you have the power to create the professional life you desire. Enjoy the process, trust yourself, and be open to new possibilities. With courage and determination, you can overcome fear and achieve the professional success you aspire to.

Most people become slaves to money when they prioritize material accumulation over their own freedom and well-being. By dedicating themselves excessively to work and sustaining a lifestyle that is often empty, they lose the true essence of happiness.

However, it is essential to keep in mind that money should not be an end in itself but rather a tool to achieve goals and build a meaningful life. Instead of submitting to the domination of money, it is important to establish a healthy relationship with it, where you have control over finances and can use resources consciously, directing them to create the desired life.

In this sense, seeking balance between financial needs and personal values is essential. Valuing experiences, relationships, and emotional well-being over excessive materialism can bring a sense of freedom and fulfillment that goes beyond the shackles of money.

Therefore, instead of becoming a slave to money, seek to be the master of your finances, using them as a means to build an abundant and meaningful life aligned with your true values and purposes.

Prioritize your personal values and goals when making financial decisions. Ask yourself what really matters to you and how you can direct your resources to support these priorities. Remember that true wealth lies in having time, freedom, and the ability to enjoy the things that bring joy and meaning to your life.

Instead of focusing solely on accumulating money, seek to find a healthy balance between work, leisure, and time for yourself. Value experiences, relationships, and personal achievements, as these are the aspects that truly enrich our lives.

Consider alternative ways to earn money that may bring greater satisfaction and purpose. Explore opportunities for entrepreneurship, self-employment, or side projects that align with your interests and passions. By doing what you love, money becomes a natural consequence of your work and no longer a source of slavery.

Remember that true success is not only about having a padded bank account, but about finding a healthy balance between work, family, leisure, and personal growth. Seek a life where you can enjoy financial freedom, but also time to dedicate to the things that truly matter.

In the end, the key is to seek personal fulfillment and happiness, rather than blindly pursuing money. By making conscious choices and aligning your actions with your deepest values, you are on the path to building a rewarding and meaningful life. Learn to live within your means and cultivate a mindset of gratitude for what you have, instead of focusing only on what is lacking. Practice responsible financial management, saving and investing wisely to create a stable financial future.

Furthermore, remember that wealth is not limited only to money. Seek to enrich your life in other ways, such as developing healthy relationships, cultivating hobbies and interests, and contributing to the community. Invest in your personal growth and in the things that bring joy and purpose to your life.

Challenge limiting beliefs and thought patterns that keep you trapped in a scarcity mindset. Cultivate an abundance mindset, recognizing the opportunities and resources available to you. Be creative in seeking solutions and be open to different ways of earning money and achieving your goals.

Also, remember to take care of yourself. Prioritize the balance between work and rest, and take care of your physical and mental health. Personal well-being is essential to enjoying a full and fulfilled life, regardless of your financial status.

Finally, remember that each person has their own journey and definition of success. Do not compare yourself to others or be influenced by external pressures. Focus on building a life that is truly meaningful and satisfying for you.

Freeing yourself from the slavery of money is an ongoing process and may require time and effort. Be kind to yourself along this journey and celebrate each achievement, no matter how small. With perseverance and determination, you can break free from the chains of money and create a life of greater freedom, purpose, and fulfillment.

CHAPTER 6.

USING MIND AND EMOTIONS TO ACHIEVE FINANCIAL FREEDOM

"Control your emotions, use your mind"

Emotions are what make us human. They make us real. The word "emotion" represents energy in motion. Be honest about your emotions and use your mind and emotions to your advantage, not against you.

Develop emotional and mental skills to make conscious and well-founded financial decisions. Instead of allowing your emotions to govern your financial choices, learn to use your rational mind to analyze the available options, consider the long-term consequences, and make wise decisions.

Cultivate a mindset of abundance and prosperity, believing that you deserve and are capable of achieving financial stability. Free yourself from limiting beliefs and fears related to money, and replace them with positive and confident thoughts.

Additionally, be aware of your emotions regarding money and learn to manage them healthily. Recognize that emotions can influence your financial behavior, but do not let them control you. Instead, use them as signals to assess your genuine needs and desires, avoiding impulsive decisions based solely on the emotions of the moment.

Practice financial discipline by setting clear goals, creating a realistic budget, and following a consistent action plan. Learn to delay immediate gratification in favor of long-term financial goals, and be willing to make temporary sacrifices for lasting benefits.

Remember that financial balance and freedom are not achieved instantly but through continuous and conscious effort. Be patient with yourself and celebrate each small victory along the way. With a combination of rational thinking, emotional management, and consistent action, you will be on the right path to achieving your financial goals and living a balanced and fulfilled financial life.

Persist in developing your emotional intelligence and practicing financial self-discipline. Learn to recognize your emotional triggers related to money and find strategies to deal with them constructively. This may include seeking support from a professional, such as a financial therapist, to help navigate deep emotional issues related to money.

Furthermore, seek continuous education about personal finance. Learn about investments, financial planning, debt management, and other relevant areas. The more knowledge you acquire, the more confident and empowered you will become to make smart financial decisions.

Stay focused on your long-term goals and be resilient in the face of setbacks. Remember that the journey toward financial stability may involve ups and downs, but the key is to keep learning, adjusting your approach when necessary, and moving toward your goal.

Finally, remember that true financial balance is not just about accumulating material wealth but about finding a balance between money and other important aspects of life, such as relationships, health, and well-being. Cultivate a holistic view of success and happiness, where money is just a part of the bigger picture.

With determination, self-awareness, and a balanced approach, you can use your emotions to think smartly about money, achieve financial freedom, and live a fulfilling and satisfying life.

Cultivate financial awareness by monitoring your expenses, creating a budget, and planning your short- and long-term financial goals. Regularly track your progress and adjust your strategies as needed.

Additionally, be mindful of your emotions regarding money. Recognize and work with any limiting beliefs or fears that may be sabotaging your financial success. Practice self-compassion and forgiveness regarding past mistakes or misguided financial decisions, and learn from them to move forward.

Utilize visualization techniques and positive affirmations to create a mindset of abundance. Imagine yourself achieving your financial goals, living a prosperous life, and enjoying financial freedom. Repeat positive affirmations related to abundance and financial success daily, strengthening your mindset and attracting the right opportunities.

Furthermore, practice gratitude for your current financial achievements. Acknowledge the blessings and resources you already have in your life. Gratitude creates a mindset of abundance and opens up space for more good things to come into your life.

By using your mind and emotions to your advantage, you can cultivate a healthy relationship with money and create the financial life you desire. Remember that you have the power to shape your financial reality through your choices, thoughts, and emotions. By acting consciously and positively, you will be on the right path to achieving financial freedom and lasting happiness. In addition to using your mind and emotions to your advantage regarding money, it is important to apply these principles to other areas of life. How you think and feel can directly influence your well-being, relationships, career, and personal goals.

Use your mind positively, cultivating constructive and optimistic thoughts. Practice mental self-care by feeding your mind with enriching information and experiences. This may include reading inspiring books, listening to motivational podcasts, seeking new knowledge, and expanding your skills.

Additionally, manage your emotions healthily. Seek to understand your emotions, identifying them and allowing yourself to feel them without suppressing them. Learn to deal with stress, anxiety, and other negative emotions through techniques such as meditation, breathing exercises, mindfulness practice, or therapeutic conversations.

Develop emotional intelligence skills, such as empathy, self-awareness, and communication skills. This will help build healthy and meaningful relationships, both personally and professionally.

Use your mind and emotions to set clear goals and direct your efforts toward achieving them. Visualize the desired success and stay motivated, even in the face of obstacles. Use positive affirmations, visualize your progress, and celebrate your achievements along the way.

Learn to manage stress and problem-solve effectively. Use your creative mind to find innovative solutions, thinking outside the box and considering different perspectives. Maintain a mindset of continuous learning, always seeking new knowledge and skills that can drive your personal and professional growth.

By using your mind and emotions to your advantage in all areas of life, you will cultivate a positive mindset, find emotional balance, and drive your personal growth. Remember that this is an ongoing process that requires practice and perseverance. Be open to learning from your mistakes and challenges, seeing them as opportunities for growth and development.

Additionally, cultivate healthy and rewarding relationships, both personally and professionally. Use your mind and emotions to build meaningful connections, demonstrating empathy, understanding, and support for others. Establish healthy boundaries and communicate clearly and respectfully.

When faced with challenges or adversities, use your mind to develop resilience and a problem-solving attitude. Instead of feeling defeated, face obstacles head-on, without letting fear dominate your life. It takes courage to take risks, to embrace the possibility of failure, and yet, to persist. For it is in this process of trial and error that we find true greatness.

Therefore, do not allow the fear of losing to stop you from pursuing your dreams. Accept it as part of the journey and turn it into strength. Remember that true defeat is not losing, but giving up. Keep pursuing your goals, even if it means facing the fear of losing. For, in the end, it is better to fight and lose than never to try and regret.

And that's why school is so foolish. In school, we learn that mistakes are bad and we are punished for making them. However, if you pay attention to the way humans learn, you will see that we learn by making mistakes. We learn to walk by falling down. If we never fall down, we will never walk. The same goes for riding a bike.

The same applies to getting rich. Unfortunately, the main reason why most people are not rich is their fear of losing. Winners are not afraid of losing. But losers are. Failures are part of the success process. People who avoid failures also avoid successes. This statement may seem paradoxical at first glance, but it is an undeniable truth. Those who are willing to risk failure are the same ones who have the chance to achieve success in its fullness.

You see, failure is not the opposite of success; it is an integral part of the path to success. Every obstacle overcome, every setback faced, and every lesson learned are essential ingredients in the cauldron of triumph.

Those who allow themselves to fail are open to growth and evolution. They understand that each failure is a learning opportunity, a chance to refine their skills and strategies. They are not discouraged by temporary defeats, but see them as steps toward ultimate success.

Those who avoid failure are also avoiding personal growth. They are content to remain within their comfort zone, where the risk of failure is minimal. However, this comfort zone is a trap disguised as security. It prevents the flourishing of talents and the discovery of true potential.

Therefore, if you truly want to achieve success, you must embrace failure as an ally, not as an enemy. Accept it as a relentless teacher, always ready to teach you valuable lessons. Be fearless in the face of adversity and see each failure as a springboard to the next level.

Remember: great achievements rarely come without their share of failure. The success stories we admire are often built on a solid foundation of trial and error. So, do not fear failure, for it is through it that you will find the true success you seek.

CHAPTER 7.

DEVELOPING FINANCIAL INTELLIGENCE

Financial intelligence is a synergy between accounting, investment, marketing, and law. Combine these four technical skills, and making money with money will be easy. Let's explore each of these areas in detail:

1. Accounting: Accounting is the foundation of financial intelligence. It involves understanding and accurately recording all financial transactions. By mastering accounting principles, you will have a clear view of personal and business finances. You will be able to analyze balance sheets, income statements, and cash flows to make informed financial decisions.

2. Investment: Investment is a powerful way to make your money work for you. By understanding different investment vehicles such as stocks, bonds, real estate, and mutual funds, you can make smart decisions to build wealth. Learning about risks and returns, diversification, and investment strategies will help maximize your gains and minimize losses.

3. Marketing: Marketing plays a key role in generating revenue and creating business opportunities. By understanding marketing principles, you can identify target markets, develop pricing, promotion, and distribution strategies, and create a unique value proposition. Effective marketing helps drive sales, increase brand visibility, and expand your customer base.

4. Law: Understanding legal principles related to finance is essential for protecting your interests and avoiding legal problems. Knowing relevant tax, contractual, and regulatory laws can help you make sound financial decisions and avoid unnecessary litigation. Knowledge of your legal rights and responsibilities is crucial for smart financial management.

By combining these four technical skills, you will have a solid foundation to conquer financial intelligence. Remember that the path to financial success requires continuous learning, adapting to changes, and financial discipline. With dedication and knowledge, you will be well-equipped to make money with money and achieve your financial goals.

For those still on the fence about the idea of working to learn something new, I offer this word of encouragement: life is much like going to the gym. The hardest part is deciding to start. Once that's done, it becomes easy. Many times, I was fearful of going to the gym, but once there, in motion, it was great. After exercising, I'm happy I decided to go.

"Everyone dreams of being rich, but they're terrified of losing money."

Most people have the desire to achieve wealth and enjoy the benefits it can bring. However, they often also have a considerable fear of losing the money they have worked hard to obtain. This fear may stem from concerns about financial security, the ability to sustain a certain standard of living, or apprehension about facing economic difficulties.

This paradox reflects human nature and the complex emotions related to money. While the desire for wealth is associated with thoughts of success, freedom, and fulfillment, the fear of losing money is linked to concerns about financial instability, failure, and a lack of control.

These conflicting emotions can be explained by psychological and social factors. Society often associates wealth with status, power, and happiness, leading people to desire to attain it. Additionally, past experiences of financial hardships, economic crises, or stories of people who lost their wealth may heighten the fear of losing money.

It is important to recognize that both the desire to be rich and the fear of losing money are natural and understandable emotions. However, it is crucial to find a healthy balance between these emotions. This involves adopting a mindful approach to dealing with money, such as seeking financial education, creating a solid financial plan, and diversifying investments.

It is also important to develop a growth mindset regarding money, understanding that financial mistakes can be opportunities for learning and growth, and that the true value of wealth lies not only in the amount of money but also in the ability to build a meaningful, balanced, and fulfilled life.

In summary, everyone dreams of being rich because of the perceived benefits that wealth can bring, but the fear of losing money is a common concern. It is important to address these emotions in a balanced and mindful way, recognizing that both the desire for wealth and the fear of losing money are normal parts of the human experience.

To deal with the fear of losing money, it is important to adopt a prudent and informed approach to finances. This may include creating a solid financial plan, setting realistic goals, and developing a diversified investment strategy. By educating yourself about basic aspects of personal finance such as budgeting, saving, and debt management, you will be better prepared to make informed financial decisions and reduce the risk of significant losses.

Additionally, it is helpful to maintain a long-term mindset when dealing with investments and financial fluctuations. Financial markets have natural ups and downs, and it is important to remain calm and not let fear dictate your investment decisions.

Working with a trusted financial advisor can help make more informed decisions and alleviate concerns related to losing money.

Another effective strategy is to build an adequate emergency fund. Having a financial safety net can reduce anxiety about potential losses, as you will have resources available to handle unforeseen expenses and emergencies.

Finally, it is important to cultivate a healthy mindset regarding money, separating your personal worth from your financial wealth. Remember that wealth does not define who you are as a person. Focus on other important aspects of life such as relationships, health, and overall happiness. In this way, you can find a healthy emotional balance regarding money and enjoy a fulfilling life regardless of your financial status.

Everyone dreams of being rich, but many have a deep fear of losing money. It's understandable, after all, money is a tool that provides us with security, comfort, and opportunities. However, it's important to understand that the fear of losing money can keep us trapped in a scarcity mindset and prevent us from achieving true wealth.

The truth is, money is a resource that is constantly in motion. Just as nature has its seasons of growth and decline, money also goes through cycles. Financial losses may be inevitable at certain times, but it is in these moments of adversity that the greatest opportunities arise.

Those who achieve financial success understand that losses are an integral part of the process. They do not allow the fear of losing money to paralyze them. Instead, they see losses as valuable lessons and opportunities for growth. They learn from mistakes, adjust their strategies, and move forward with renewed determination.

It is important to remember that true financial power lies not only in accumulating wealth but also in the ability to recover and adapt in the face of losses. Learning to deal with the fear of losing money requires a mindset of abundance and confidence in one's own potential.

To overcome this fear, it is essential to educate yourself financially. Learn about investments, risk management strategies, and portfolio diversification. Develop a solid financial plan and be prepared to face ups and downs. Seek guidance from qualified professionals, such as financial advisors, to help you make informed decisions.

Remember that money is a tool to achieve your goals and live the life you desire. Do not let the fear of losing money prevent you from seeking opportunities and realizing your dreams. Be courageous, willing to take calculated risks, and prepared to learn from defeats. In this way, you will be on the right path to achieving true wealth and prosperity.

CHAPTER 8.

BALANCE AND FOCUS: LESSONS FROM THE GENIUSES OF HISTORY

True geniuses have made significant contributions in different areas of knowledge throughout history, constantly maintaining balance and focus, seemingly immune to distractions and obstacles that might arise in their path. Like a tightrope walker on a tightrope, keeping each step firm and stable even when strong winds blow around them, you must maintain balance, focusing on the point ahead and blocking out any external interference. Here's a brief summary of each of these focused geniuses:

1. Thomas Edison: One of the most prolific inventors in history, Edison is known for inventing the electric light bulb and developing the electrical power distribution system. He recorded over a thousand patents during his lifetime.

2. Plato and Socrates: Plato was one of the most influential philosophers of ancient Greece and founded the Academy of Athens. His teacher, Socrates, was one of the most important thinkers in Western philosophy, known for his Socratic method of questioning.

3. René Descartes: Considered one of the fathers of modern philosophy, Descartes is known for his famous words "I think, therefore I am." He made important contributions to mathematics, philosophy, and science.

4. Hippocrates: Known as the father of modern medicine, Hippocrates was a Greek physician who established medical ethics and developed the Hippocratic Oath, still used by doctors today.

5. Nikola Tesla: One of the greatest inventors and engineers in history, Tesla contributed to the development of alternating current, improved wireless energy transmission technology, and invented the induction motor.

6. Gregor Mendel: Known as the father of genetics, Mendel was an Augustinian friar who conducted pioneering studies with peas and discovered the laws of genetic inheritance, which are fundamental to understanding modern genetics.

7. Leonardo da Vinci: Italian Renaissance man, da Vinci was a polymath genius, excelling in areas such as painting, sculpture, architecture, science, mathematics, and engineering. His most famous works include the "Mona Lisa" and "The Last Supper."

8. Nicolaus Copernicus: Polish astronomer, Copernicus developed the heliocentric theory, which stated that the Earth revolves around the Sun, challenging prevailing geocentric beliefs at the time.

9. Isaac Newton: English physicist, mathematician, and astronomer, Newton is known for his laws of motion and universal gravitation. His work "Mathematical Principles of Natural Philosophy" is considered a milestone in modern science.

10. Albert Einstein: German theoretical physicist, Einstein is known for his theory of relativity, which revolutionized physics. He also made significant contributions to the development of quantum mechanics.

These geniuses left a lasting legacy in their respective fields, and their discoveries and inventions continue to influence and inspire future generations.

These remarkable individuals not only left a legacy of knowledge and innovation, but many of them also demonstrated balance and focus in their lives. While each of them faced challenges and obstacles, they found ways to stay centered and focused on their passions and goals.

These extraordinary individuals understood the importance of cultivating a balanced mindset, which involves taking care of their mental, emotional, and physical health. They recognized that personal well-being is essential for lasting success and for achieving their goals.

For many of these geniuses, balance came in the form of pursuing different areas of interest beyond their primary disciplines. Leonardo da Vinci, for example, was a accomplished artist but also engaged in scientific studies and engineering. He believed that the fusion of arts and sciences was crucial for a creative and innovative mind.

Additionally, these geniuses valued time for reflection and contemplation. Socrates and Plato, for example, were known for their dialogue and questioning practices, constantly seeking wisdom and truth. They recognized the importance of stepping away from the distractions of the external world and dedicating time to think deeply about philosophical and moral issues.

Another crucial aspect of balance that these geniuses addressed was the ability to adapt to change. Isaac Newton, for example, was a brilliant scientist but also had periods of introspection and contemplation. He understood that mental flexibility and the ability to adjust to circumstances were crucial for progress and innovation.

Furthermore, many of these geniuses found inspiration in nature. They realized the importance of connecting with the world around them and found motivation in its beauty and complexity.

This connection with nature helped nurture their creativity and sense of purpose.

Finally, these geniuses also understood the importance of setting clear goals and focusing on achieving them. They did not allow themselves to be distracted by temptations of quick and easy money, which are often risky and uncertain. Instead, they kept their attention on their goals and worked diligently to achieve them.

By learning from these geniuses, we can understand that the pursuit of success and wealth should not only be about accumulating material riches. It is crucial to find balance in all areas of our lives and remain focused on our passions and goals. Only then can we achieve our own version of success and lasting happiness.

Remember that balance and focus are skills that can be developed and honed over time. With dedication and practice, you can find the balance needed to pursue your dreams and achieve the wealth you desire, not only financially but also in terms of personal fulfillment and overall well-being.

If you desire to achieve wealth, it is crucial to maintain focus and adopt a strategic approach. Instead of spreading your resources and energies across various areas, it is more advantageous to focus on a few promising opportunities. This approach differs from that adopted by lower-income individuals or even the middle class, who tend to spread their investments across multiple areas.

By concentrating your efforts on a few baskets, you can dedicate time, energy, and resources more efficiently. This allows you to closely monitor progress and take corrective measures when necessary. In this way, your chances of success increase, as you are directing your resources to the best opportunities.

However, it is important to emphasize that this strategy does not mean putting all your eggs in one basket. Diversifying your investments within a few strategic areas is essential to reduce risks and maximize return potential. The balance between focus and diversification is essential for a smart approach to seeking wealth.

Remember that the path to wealth involves discipline, perseverance, and continuous learning. Be willing to adapt your strategy based on changing circumstances and opportunities. By staying focused, committed, and open to adjustments, you increase your chances of achieving your financial goals.

This means that you should invest your time, energy, and money in a few opportunities that have high potential for return. Do not be distracted by the temptations of making quick and easy money, which are often risky and uncertain. Instead, choose a niche market, a product or service, or a skill that you can master and that has demand. Then, dedicate yourself to learning everything you can about it, improving your offering, and building your reputation and network. This way, you will increase your chances of becoming an expert, a leader, or an innovator in your field.

You should invest a portion of your earnings in assets that generate passive income, meaning that they do not depend on your time or effort to generate profit. These assets can be stocks, real estate investment trusts, government bonds, or other types of investments that pay dividends, interest, or rents. This way, you will be able to increase your wealth without having to work more for it. You will also be able to take advantage of the power of compound interest, which makes your money grow exponentially over time. This way, you will be able to achieve financial independence, and have more freedom and quality of life.

...

Awaken the financial genius within you. It is dormant because our culture teaches us to believe that the love of money is the root of all evil. It encourages us to learn a profession so that we can work for money, but it does not teach us to make money work for us. It teaches us not to worry about our financial future, the government or the company will take care of us when retirement comes. Learn from mistakes, recognizing that not all steps will be perfect. Face challenges as opportunities for growth and keep moving forward. Be alert to trends and changes in the field you want to thrive in financially. This may involve regular research, reading relevant books, and participating in industry events.

Avoid distractions that can divert your attention and compromise your financial progress. This should include reducing time on social media, limiting interruptions, and creating a quiet work environment. Stay focused.

CHAPTER 9.

THE POWER OF SELF-DISCIPLINE ON THE JOURNEY TO WEALTH

Many people choose not to be rich. For about 95% of the population, being rich is "too much hassle." So they come up with things like "I'm not interested in money," "money isn't everything," "I'll never be rich," "I don't need to worry, I'm still young," "When I have some money, I'll think about my future," or "My husband/wife handles the finances." The problem with these statements is that they rob people who think this way of two things: one, time, which is our most precious asset; and two, learning. Just because you don't have money, that's no excuse not to learn. But it's a choice we make every day, the choice of what to do with our time, with our money, and with what we put into our heads. And the power of choice. We all have a choice. I chose to be rich and make that choice every day.

Listening is more important than speaking. If that weren't true, God wouldn't have given us two ears and only one mouth. Too many people think with their mouths instead of listening to assimilate new ideas and possibilities. Effective communication depends on attentive listening. This avoids jumping to premature conclusions.

It's important to filter the opinions we receive and not listen to people who have a negative mindset about money and investments. While they may be nice people, they tend to be pessimistic and attract undesirable outcomes.

When it comes to financial matters, it's common to hear these people always warning about problems and reasons why things don't work. However, it's essential to remember that those who accept this pessimistic information also have a negative mindset. As the saying goes, "birds of a feather flock together."

Instead of being influenced by these pessimistic perspectives, it's crucial to seek knowledge and guidance from reliable and positive sources in the financial field. Look for mentors, experts, and successful people who can provide valuable insights and encouragement. Surround yourself with individuals who believe in the potential for growth and financial success.

Remember that a positive mindset plays a crucial role in achieving financial goals. By believing in yourself and your abilities, you're more likely to make confident decisions and attract prosperity. Cultivate an optimistic mindset and focus on solutions and opportunities rather than dwelling on challenges.

Don't let others' negativity prevent you from pursuing financial success. Stay true to your goals, learn from the experiences of those who have already succeeded, and remain determined to reach your full financial potential. Believe in yourself and the possibility of creating a prosperous and abundant life.

It's true that what you study and learn has a significant impact on your life. Just as the phrase "you are what you eat" emphasizes the importance of healthy eating for physical well-being, the phrase "you become what you study" highlights the influence of knowledge and learning on your mindset and development.

Therefore, it's crucial to carefully select what you study and absorb into your mind. Your mind is a powerful tool, and what you put into it will shape your thinking, actions, and ability to achieve your goals. Seek knowledge and information that are positive, enriching, and aligned with your values and goals.

The lack of self-discipline is a factor that contributes to the financial decline of many lottery winners and people who receive salary increases. It's the lack of control and self-discipline that leads these people to spend impulsively on temporary luxuries, such as new cars or extravagant trips.

Furthermore, people with low self-esteem and little tolerance for financial pressure struggle to achieve wealth. This is not because other people are mean, but because these individuals lack internal control and discipline to deal with the financial adversities that arise in their lives.

It's important to recognize that people with poor habits often face financial difficulties. A common example is the habit of withdrawing money from their savings indiscriminately, without considering the long-term consequences.

Therefore, to achieve financial prosperity, it's essential to cultivate healthy habits and discipline. This involves learning to control your impulses, developing a solid financial plan, and adopting responsible financial practices. By choosing to study and learn about personal finance, investments, and financial management skills, you'll strengthen your mindset and increase your chances of financial success.

"If a person doesn't master the power of self-discipline, it's better not to try to become rich."

Self-discipline is the ability to control your impulses, emotions, and habits, and to act according to your goals and values. It's an essential skill for anyone who wants to become rich because without it, you won't be able to maintain the focus, persistence, and consistency needed to achieve success. Without self-discipline, you'll be swayed by distractions, temptations, and excuses that sabotage your progress. You'll also spend more than you earn and won't have the ability to save and invest your money. You'll miss opportunities, deadlines, and commitments, and harm your reputation and credibility. That's why if you don't master the power of self-discipline, it's better not to try to become rich.

But how do you develop self-discipline? The answer is simple: by practicing. Self-discipline is like a muscle that strengthens with use. You can start with small challenges, like waking up earlier, exercising, or avoiding sweets. Then, you can increase the level of difficulty, such as learning a new language, taking an online course, or starting a personal project. The important thing is to set clear and realistic goals and to achieve them with determination and responsibility. You should also monitor your progress and celebrate your achievements. This way, you'll create the habit of self-discipline and feel more confident and motivated to face bigger challenges that arise on your path to wealth.

When I wanted to buy a Porsche or a Mercedes, the easiest way was to go to the bank manager and get a loan. Instead of worrying about the liability column, I decided to focus on the asset column. As usual, I used my desire to consume to inspire and motivate my financial genius to invest. We constantly worry about getting the things we want instead of focusing on creating money. It's easier in the short term but harder in the long run. It's a bad habit we fall into as individuals and as a nation. Remember, the easiest path often becomes the roughest, and the hard path often becomes smoother. This means you shouldn't seek shortcuts, magic formulas, or miraculous solutions to get rich. These seemingly easy paths can turn out to be traps, scams, or illusions that can cost you dearly financially and morally. Instead, you should follow the path of ethics, work, and continuous learning, which may seem tough and time-consuming but brings solid and lasting results. This path also becomes smoother as you gain more knowledge, experience, and confidence and as you reap the rewards of your efforts. So, remember: the easiest path often becomes the roughest, and the hard path often becomes smoother.

To be the master of money, you need to be smarter than it. Then money will do what you command. It will obey you. Instead of being a slave, you will be the master. That's financial intelligence. It's the ability to understand how money works and to use it to your advantage. It's the skill of managing your personal finances, budgeting, saving, investing, and planning your financial future. It's knowledge of laws, taxes, interest, and opportunities in the financial market. It's the art of negotiating, selling, buying, and creating value. It's the science of calculating risks, analyzing scenarios, and making rational decisions. It's the wisdom of balancing your needs, desires, and dreams. It's the virtue of being generous, grateful, and mindful. To be the master of money, you need to be smarter than it. Then money will do what you command. It will obey you. Instead of being a slave, you will be the master. That's financial intelligence.

Whenever you feel "lack" or "scarcity" of something, give away, beforehand, what you desire and it will return to you in abundance. This is true for money, smiles, love, friendship. I know that often this is the last thing one wants to do, but for me, it has always worked. This is the law of abundance, which governs the universe. Everything you give, you receive back. Everything you sow, you reap. Everything you emanate, you attract. The universe is a mirror, reflecting your energy, your vibration, and your frequency. When you give, you demonstrate trust in divine providence, knowing that there is enough for everyone, acknowledging your prosperity. When you give, you open up space to receive, you create a flow of abundance, you activate your gratitude. When you give, you connect with the source of all wealth, which is love. Love is the most powerful force in the universe, capable of transforming any situation, realizing any dream, overcoming any obstacle. Whenever you feel a "lack" or "scarcity" of something, give away, beforehand, what you desire and it will return to you in abundance. This is true for money, smiles, love, friendship. I know that often this is the last thing one wants to do, but for me, it has always worked. And I'm sure it will work for you too.

But how to give if you don't have what to give? The answer is simple: you always have something to give. You can give your time, your talent, your knowledge, your service, your support, your affection. You can give a hug, a compliment, advice, a prayer, a smile. You can give a book, clothes, a toy, food, medicine. You can give what you can, how you can, when you can. The important thing is that you give with joy, generosity, and sincerity. The important thing is that you give without expecting anything in return, without seeking recognition, without demanding reward. The important thing is that you give from the heart, from the soul, from the spirit. God will always be blessing you, believe in that.

"The poor are more greedy than the rich."

This is a controversial statement, but it has a grain of truth. The poor are more greedy than the rich because they live in scarcity, deprivation, limitation. They don't have enough to satisfy their basic needs, let alone fulfill their desires and dreams. They feel unjust, frustrated, and envious. They want to have more, but they don't know how to get it. They think money is the solution to all their problems, but they lack the necessary financial education to manage it well. They spend more than they earn, get into debt, and sink deeper into poverty. They cling to what they have and don't share with anyone. They are selfish, petty, and stingy.

Most of the rich, on the other hand, are less greedy than the poor because they live in abundance, prosperity, freedom. They have enough to satisfy their basic needs, and also to fulfill their desires and dreams. They feel grateful, happy, and generous. They want to have more, but they know how to get it. They understand that money is a tool to create value, to make a difference, to help others. They have the necessary financial education to manage it well. They earn more than they spend, invest, and multiply their wealth. They detach from what they have and share with those in need. They are altruistic, benevolent, and magnanimous. Be a giver, throughout my life, over all these years, whenever I felt the need for money or even assistance, I would look deep into my heart for what I wanted and decided to give it away beforehand. By doing so, what I gave away always returned to me.

I have found that the more sincerely I teach those eager to learn, the more I learn. If you want to learn about money, teach someone. A torrent of new ideas and more subtle distinctions will emerge.

There are powers in this world much stronger than us. You can get there by yourself, but you'll get there faster with the help of higher powers. All you need to do is be generous with what you have, and the higher powers will be generous with you.

These higher powers are the invisible forces that govern the universe, which are beyond our understanding, that transcend our reality. They can be called God, Spirit, Energy, Source, Life, or any other name you prefer. They are the origin of all creation, of all existence, of all manifestation. They are the essence of everything that is, everything that was, and everything that will be. They are love, wisdom, and supreme power.

Regarding God, I believe it is the greatest of the higher powers, the creator of all others, the father of all things. It is what gives us life, sustains us, guides us, loves us, forgives us, saves us, knows us, hears us, responds to us. God is what blesses us, protects us, enlightens us. It is our refuge, our fortress, our hope. God is everything to us, and we are everything to God.

The existence of the creator is an undeniable truth, revealed in all its work. Just look at nature, the sky, the sea, the mountains, the flowers, the animals, to see their beauty, their harmony, their perfection. Just look at the human being, at their body, their mind, their soul, to see their complexity, their intelligence, their divinity. Just look at history, science, art, culture, to see their evolution, their creativity, their manifestation. Just look at your heart, your feelings, your emotions, to see your love, your kindness, your presence. God is in everything and everyone, and everything and everyone is in God.

You and only you have the power to determine the destiny of your life in all aspects. This means that you are solely responsible for your success or failure, for your wealth or poverty, for your happiness or unhappiness. You cannot blame anyone or anything for your circumstances, your choices, your consequences. You cannot victimize yourself, lament, resign. You have to take control of your life, take the reins of your destiny, make a difference in your world. You have to define your goals, outline your plans, execute your actions. You have to seek knowledge, develop skills, apply strategies. You have to overcome your fears, face your challenges, overcome your obstacles. You have to believe in yourself, trust your potential, value your talents. You and only you have the power to determine the destiny of your life in all aspects, including financial.

I also believe that the mind and time must be better managed in order to achieve success. These are the two most valuable resources you possess, and you must use them wisely. Your mind is your instrument of creation, solution, transformation. It is with it that you think, learn, innovate. It is with it that you imagine, dream, accomplish. Your mind is your greatest asset, and you must take care of it, feed it, exercise it. You must read, study, research. You must question, analyze, criticize. You must meditate, reflect, inspire. You must expand your mind, not limit it.

Your time is your most scarce resource, and you must use it efficiently. It is with it that you live, work, have fun. It is with it that you plan, execute, evaluate. Your time is your most precious asset, and you must value it, organize it, make the most of it. You must set priorities, define goals, meet deadlines. You must eliminate distractions, avoid procrastination, optimize processes. You must balance work and leisure, rest and activity, routine and novelty. You must live your time, not waste it.

"The Consciousness of Success and Overcoming the Impossible"

Before success comes into anyone's life, it is inevitable to face many temporary defeats and perhaps even some failures. When defeat strikes someone, the easiest and most logical reaction is to give up, and that's exactly what most people do.

However, when riches begin to flow, they come with such surprising speed and abundance that we wonder where they were during all those years of scarcity. Success is achieved by those who have a consciousness oriented towards success, while failure comes to those who, indifferent, resign themselves to failure.

One of the main weaknesses of human beings is the tendency of the common man to become familiar with the word "impossible." But it is important to understand that a strong man can be defeated by a child with a defined purpose. By changing your thought patterns regarding the meaning of your task, it is often possible to achieve what would apparently be impossible.

Therefore, it is fundamental to develop a positive and resolute consciousness towards success, abandoning the limiting mentality of the impossible. Believing in yourself, staying focused, and being willing to overcome obstacles are essential pillars for achieving what many would consider impossible.

By cultivating this mindset, you will be able to impart to others your faith and persistence, and accomplish what many consider "impossible." Everything the human mind can conceive and believe, can be achieved.

Dreams become reality when desire is transformed into concrete action. By asking life for great gifts and stimulating it, you will be blessed with them. All human beings who grasp the purpose of money yearn for it, but mere yearning does not bring riches. However, by desiring with an obsessive mindset, planning definite methods and means to acquire them, and sustaining these plans with a persistence that knows no failure, riches will come.

Therefore, it is important to feed your mind with positive thoughts, visualize your goals clearly, and act consistently towards them. Believe in the power of the impossible, stay determined and perseverant, and you will pave the way for success and the fulfillment of your dreams.

Along this journey, you may encounter people who doubt your aspirations and try to discourage you. However, it is important to remember that your beliefs and determination are more powerful than any negative opinion. Stay true to your dreams and goals, even in the face of adversity.

Moreover, do not underestimate the power of action. Dreams and desires are just the starting point; they need to be turned into concrete actions. Set clear goals, devise an action plan, and take consistent steps towards them. With each small achievement, you will build positive momentum that will propel you forward.

Remember that failure is part of the process. See it as an opportunity for learning and growth, rather than a sign to give up. Learn from your mistakes, adjust your approach, and move forward with renewed determination.

In the end, by pursuing the impossible, you will discover an inner strength that you never knew you had. The journey itself is transformative, shaping your character and teaching you valuable lessons along the way.

So, embrace the possibility of the impossible, keep the flame of hope and perseverance alive in your heart. With faith, persistence, and consistent action, you will achieve results beyond what you ever imagined possible. Believe in yourself and the unlimited power that exists within you to conquer the impossible.

"Seven Gifts to Prosper"

1. Establish in your mind the specific value of money you wish to acquire. It's not enough to simply state, 'I want a lot of money.' Be clear and precise about the desired amount.

2. Decide precisely what you are willing to offer in exchange for the money you wish to acquire. This may include your time, skills, knowledge, or resources. For example, you may be willing to work overtime, acquire new skills, or invest in a business to reach your financial goal. Having clarity about what you are willing to give in exchange for the money you desire can help you make informed decisions and achieve your goals more effectively.

3. Set a specific deadline for when you want to acquire the money you aim for. Having a defined date in mind can help you focus and work towards your financial goal. Setting a realistic and

achievable deadline can motivate you to take consistent steps to reach your financial goal.

4. Develop a concrete plan to fulfill your desire and start acting immediately, regardless of whether you feel fully prepared or not to put the plan into practice. Having a well-defined plan can help you focus and take consistent steps towards your goal. Don't wait until you feel 100% ready to start - often, action is what leads us to feel more prepared and confident. Start with small steps and adjust your plan as needed along the way.

5. Draft an objective and concise statement, specifying the amount of money you want to acquire, setting a deadline to achieve it, determining what you are willing to offer in exchange for the money, and clearly describing the plan you will follow to accumulate it.

6. Resilience is the ability to bounce back from adversity and move forward, even in the face of challenges and difficulties. It is an important attribute for success, as it allows people to face obstacles and overcome setbacks without giving up on their goals. Developing resilience may involve practices such as taking care of your physical and mental health, cultivating positive relationships, practicing gratitude and optimism, and seeking support when needed.

7. Have faith in yourself and your abilities. With a positive and confident attitude, you can achieve success in your goals. Believe in your potential and don't give up in the face of challenges.

When faith is joined with thought, the subconscious immediately picks up the vibration, translating it into its spiritual equivalent. By transmitting your faith to the Infinite Intelligence, as in the case of prayer, you may find comfort and guidance in times of uncertainty. Connecting with something greater than ourselves can help us find strength and purpose in our lives. It is important to remember that faith is a personal journey, and each must find their own way to connect with Infinite Intelligence.

The repetition of positive affirmations can help develop the emotion of faith voluntarily. By repeating affirmations to yourself, you are sending a clear message to your subconscious about what you want to achieve. Over time, these affirmations can become part of your inner belief and help you act in accordance with your goals. It is important to choose affirmations that are meaningful to you and repeat them regularly for the best results.

By convincing your subconscious that you believe you will receive what you desire, you can trigger a series of positive events. Your subconscious will act according to your beliefs and give back to you the faith in the form of definite plans to achieve your goals. It is important to keep in mind that faith is not just a feeling but also an action. By acting according to your plans and working towards your goals, you can turn your faith into reality.

Faith is a powerful element that can transform our lives in many ways. It is the starting point for wealth accumulation and the basis of all miracles and mysteries that defy scientific understanding. Faith is the only antidote to failure and can help us overcome obstacles and achieve our goals. When mixed with prayer, faith allows direct communication with Infinite Intelligence and can turn our thoughts into reality. It is a powerful tool that allows us to master and use the cosmic force of Infinite Intelligence.

Faith is the eternal elixir that infuses life, strength, and movement into thought impulses. The human mind is constantly attracting vibrations that harmonize with its dominant thoughts. This means that our thoughts have the power to influence our reality and attract to us what we desire. It is important to keep in mind that our thoughts have energy and can affect our environment and the people around us. By cultivating positive thoughts and focusing on what we desire, we can attract positive vibrations and create a more favorable reality for ourselves.

It may seem difficult to imagine yourself possessing money before actually having it. However, it is important to remember that those who have amassed great fortunes began with dreams, hopes, desires, and plans. Before acquiring wealth, they dedicated time and energy to visualize their goals and devise a plan to achieve them. Believing in yourself and your abilities is an important step on the path to financial success.

It is important to understand that, to accumulate large amounts of wealth, you must have a strong desire for money and truly believe in your ability to obtain it.

The most influential leaders in the world have always been those who have been able to master and utilize the intangible and invisible forces of yet-to-be-realized opportunities. They have transformed these forces, or thought impulses, into skyscrapers, cities, factories, airplanes, automobiles, and all kinds of utilities that make life more enjoyable. Do not allow anyone to negatively influence you. The Wright brothers and Santos Dumont dreamed of a machine capable of flying. They did not let negative opinions discourage them, and as a result, the airplane was invented. Thomas Edison dreamed of creating a light bulb that could be powered by electricity. He worked tirelessly on his experiments and finally succeeded in inventing the electric light bulb, forever changing the way we illuminate our homes and cities. Their names will be eternal because they dreamed and turned their dreams into structured thoughts. They left a lasting legacy, inspiring future generations to follow in their footsteps and believe in the power of dreams.

"No one is ready for something until they believe they can achieve it."

Any idea, plan, or purpose can be fixed in the mind through constant repetition of thought. It is important to have self-confidence and believe in yourself so that these thoughts become reality. This is one of the main goals set in life, and I will never give up trying to achieve it until I develop the necessary self-confidence. No wealth or position can last long without being built upon truth and justice. Therefore, I commit to not engage in any transaction that does not benefit all parties involved. I believe that, by acting with integrity and ethics, I can achieve my goals fairly and lastingly. I will achieve success by attracting to myself the forces I wish to use and the cooperation of other people. I will make others serve me by demonstrating my willingness to serve them. I will eliminate negative feelings such as hatred, envy, selfishness, and cynicism by cultivating love for humanity. I know that a negative attitude towards others will never lead me to success. Instead, I will seek to build positive and collaborative relationships based on mutual respect and empathy.

CHAPTER 10.

DEVELOPING THE WINNING MINDSET: THE POWER OF SELF-SUGGESTION AND BELIEF IN YOURSELF

"The principle of self-suggestion"

Self-confidence is a powerful force that propels us towards success. It's important to cultivate this confidence by believing in our abilities and working to further develop them. With the right mindset, we can achieve our goals and conquer life's battles.

Just as a skilled musician can extract beautiful melodies from the strings of a violin, you too can awaken the The principle of self-suggestion is a powerful tool that allows us to influence our thoughts and behaviors. By repeating positive affirmations and visualizing desired outcomes, we can program our minds to achieve our goals. It's essential to use self-suggestion consciously and intentionally, to direct our thoughts and actions towards success.

In life's battles, it's not always the strongest or fastest man who emerges victorious. In the end, triumph belongs to those who believe in their ability to win! Belief in oneself empowers a person to overcome obstacles and face challenges with determination and perseverance.

By cultivating this mindset of confidence and self-esteem, we are able to confront challenges with a positive and resilient attitude. Believing in our ability to succeed motivates us to persist in the face of difficulties and seek creative solutions to achieve our goals.

Remember that self-suggestion is a powerful tool but requires practice and consistency. By repeating positive affirmations about our abilities and visualizing success in our minds, we strengthen our confidence and increase our chances of achieving what we desire.

Therefore, believe in yourself, nurture positive thoughts, and use self-suggestion as an ally to direct your efforts towards success. With determination and a winning mindset, you will be able to overcome any challenge that comes your way. When facing challenges, maintain the conviction that you have the skills and resources necessary to overcome them. Visualize yourself achieving your goals, experiencing the feeling of victory and fulfillment. This powerful visualization strengthens your mindset and helps create a clear path towards success.

Furthermore, practice self-discipline and perseverance. Be willing to put effort and hard work into your goals. Remember that success rarely comes overnight but is built through consistent actions and unwavering determination.

Surround yourself with positive and inspiring influences. Read motivational books, listen to inspiring lectures, and connect with people who share your winning mindset. These experiences and interactions fuel your motivation and reinforce your personal belief in your potential.

However, be prepared to face setbacks and obstacles along the way. See challenges as opportunities for growth and learning. Each obstacle overcome strengthens your resilience and empowers you to face even greater challenges in the future.

Remember that you are the author of your own story. With the right combination of self-suggestion, confidence, self-discipline, and perseverance, you can achieve great feats and realize your boldest dreams. Keep your focus on your goal, believe in yourself, and move forward with determination. Success is within your reach.

Never underestimate the power of your own potential. We all have unique abilities and talents that can be developed and enhanced. With determination and effort, we can achieve great accomplishments and surpass our own expectations. Remember that success is not just a matter of luck or destiny but the result of hard work and dedication. Believe in yourself and your abilities, and you will be able to achieve anything you desire.

"The strength of faith"

Faith is a powerful force that can give us the courage and determination to face life's challenges. When we believe in something wholeheartedly, we are able to overcome obstacles and achieve our goals. Faith gives us the confidence to move forward, even when things seem difficult. It's important to cultivate faith in ourselves and our abilities so that we can face the world with confidence and determination.

The essence of the teachings and accomplishments of Christ, often interpreted as 'miracles,' was faith. If there are phenomena like 'miracles,' they are produced through the state of mind known as faith. Faith is a powerful force that can lead us to achieve incredible things and overcome seemingly insurmountable obstacles. Faith gives us the courage and determination to face life's challenges and achieve our goals. When we believe in something with all our hearts, we are able to overcome obstacles and accomplish amazing things. It's important to cultivate faith in ourselves and our abilities so that we can face the world with confidence and determination. With faith, we can achieve great accomplishments and surpass our own expectations.

Consider the example of Mahatma Gandhi from India, who demonstrated the power of faith in an impressive manner. Gandhi was one of the greatest examples of the possibilities of faith, controlling a potential power greater than anyone else of his time, even without possessing traditional instruments of power such as money, warships, soldiers, and weapons. Gandhi had no riches, no fixed home, not even a suit to wear, yet he possessed great power. How did he achieve this? Through his understanding of the principle of faith and his ability to convey that faith to the minds of two hundred million people. Gandhi was able to inspire and mobilize millions of people through his faith and determination. He believed in his ideals and worked tirelessly to promote them, even in the face of great adversity. His faith gave him the strength and courage to face challenges and overcome obstacles, and his ability to convey that faith to others was crucial to his success. Gandhi's example shows us the power of faith and how it can lead us to achieve great accomplishments.

Wealth begins as a thought! Before it materializes, wealth is conceived in our minds, through our thoughts and ideas. It's important to cultivate a positive mindset focused on our goals so that we can turn our dreams into reality. Our thoughts have great power over our lives. When we think positively and focus on our goals, we are able to attract opportunities and create favorable conditions for success. On the other hand, if we let ourselves be carried away by negative and defeatist thoughts, we may end up sabotaging our own chances of success. It's important to cultivate a positive mindset and believe in our abilities so that we can achieve wealth and success. Remember that wealth is not just a matter of money or material possessions, but also includes personal satisfaction and the fulfillment of our dreams and goals. Cultivate a positive mindset and work hard to achieve your goals, and you will be able to create the wealth you desire in your life. Believe in yourself and your abilities, and you will be able to turn your dreams into reality.

The amount of success we can achieve is limited only by our own mind and the thoughts we set in motion. Faith is a key element for success and can be strengthened through instructions given to our subconscious. It's important to remember that to gain, one must first give. Both poverty and wealth are results of the faith we have in ourselves and our abilities. Faith is a powerful force that can lead us to achieve great accomplishments. When we believe in ourselves and our abilities, we are able to overcome obstacles and face challenges with determination and perseverance. It's important to cultivate faith in ourselves, believing in our abilities and working to further develop them. With the right mindset, we can achieve our goals and create the life we desire, whether it be rich or modest.

Make the deepest part of your mind work for you. Support it with the power of emotions, and you will see that the combination is impressive. Self-suggestion is the suggestion we make to ourselves and is the instrument of communication between the conscious and subconscious parts of the mind. By using self-suggestion consciously and intentionally, we can influence our thoughts and behaviors, achieving our goals more effectively. Creative visualization is a powerful tool that can help us achieve our goals. Through the repetition of positive affirmations and the visualization of desired outcomes, we can program our minds for success. It's important to emotionalize these affirmations and visualizations with faith so that they have a deeper impact on our subconscious. With practice, we can develop the ability to use self-suggestion to achieve our goals and realize our dreams.

Through the dominant thoughts that we allow to remain in our conscious mind, whether they are negative or positive, the principle of self-suggestion voluntarily reaches the subconscious, influencing it with these thoughts. To achieve meaningful results, it's important to learn to reach the subconscious with thoughts and words emotionalized with faith. Self-suggestion is a powerful tool that can help us influence our thoughts and behaviors. By using positive affirmations and creative visualizations, we can program our minds for success. It's important to emotionalize these affirmations and visualizations with faith so that they have a deeper impact on our subconscious. With practice, we can develop the ability to use self-suggestion to achieve our goals and realize our dreams. Your ability to use the principle of self-suggestion will largely depend on your ability to focus on a given desire until it becomes a burning obsession.

The individual has the ability to master himself and the environment around him, as he has the ability to exert influence over the subconscious. This means that through conscious control of our thoughts and actions, we can shape our lives and the world around us. By influencing our subconscious, we can change our behavior patterns and achieve our goals.

An educated individual is not necessarily one who possesses a vast amount of general or specialized knowledge. An educated individual is one who has developed their mental faculties to such an extent that they can acquire what they desire, or its equivalent, without infringing upon the rights of others. Sufficiently "Ignorant" to Make a Fortune. During the First World War, a Chicago newspaper published articles in which Henry Ford was called an "ignorant pacifist," among other claims. Ford protested against these claims and sued the newspaper for defamation. In court, the newspaper's lawyers argued in defense and called Ford to testify, aiming to prove to the jury that he was ignorant. They asked many questions, all with the goal of proving that, although he possessed considerable specialized knowledge in automobile manufacturing, he was generally ignorant. Ford, however, handled the situation skillfully. When asked a question he didn't know the answer to, he simply replied, "Don't I have a line of men at my desk waiting to provide me with information on any subject I want? Why should I clutter my mind with general facts when I have men around me who can provide any knowledge I need?" This response clearly demonstrated that Ford understood the value of specialized knowledge and task delegation. He may not have had a wide range of general knowledge, but he knew how to acquire the knowledge he needed to succeed in his endeavors. He knew how to surround himself with competent people and rely on them to provide the necessary information. This allowed him to focus on his own areas of expertise and achieve great accomplishments. Everyone in the courtroom understood that it was the response not of an ignorant person, but of an educated man.

Anyone who knows where to find the knowledge they need and knows how to organize that knowledge into action plans is an educated person. With the help of his "Master Mind" group, Henry Ford had access to all the specialized knowledge he needed to become one of the wealthiest men in the United States. It wasn't necessary for him to have all that knowledge in his own mind. This demonstrates the importance of knowing how to acquire and utilize specialized knowledge. It's not necessary to have all the knowledge in your own mind, but it's important to know where to find the knowledge you need and how to organize it into action plans. By doing so, you can achieve great accomplishments and success in your endeavors.

Thomas A. Edison had only three months of formal education in his life, but that didn't stop him from being educated or dying wealthy. Similarly, Henry Ford had little more than the second year of elementary school, yet he still achieved great financial success. Specialized knowledge is one of the most common and accessible forms of service one can find. If you doubt this, just check the payroll of any university. This demonstrates that formal education is not the only way to acquire knowledge and succeed in life. Specialized knowledge can be acquired in many different ways and is highly valued in the job market. It's important to know how to acquire and utilize specialized knowledge to achieve your goals and succeed in your endeavors.

Individuals successful in all professional fields continue to acquire specialized knowledge throughout their careers.

The bottom is a discouraging, gloomy, and unfavorable place for anyone. That's why I've dedicated so much time to explaining how starting from the bottom can be avoided through proper planning. The idea is paramount. Specialized knowledge can easily be found around the corner. This means that with proper planning and a clear idea of what you want to achieve, it's possible to avoid starting from the bottom and progress towards success. Specialized knowledge is a valuable tool in this process and can be easily acquired if you know where to look. With the right combination of planning, ideas, and specialized knowledge, you can achieve your goals and succeed in your endeavors. Open your mind to instruction that comes from experience and contact with other minds. Knowledge is the key to wealth, as long as you know which path to follow. All the opportunities you need in life are waiting in your imagination. Imagination is the workshop of the mind, capable of turning mental energy into achievements and wealth. It is said that humans can create anything they can imagine. By using your imagination and acquiring the necessary knowledge, you can turn your ideas into reality and achieve wealth and success. It's important to know which path to follow and have a clear vision of your goals in order to make the most of the opportunities that arise. With the right combination of imagination, knowledge, and action, you can achieve great accomplishments and create the life you desire.

The only limitation of the human being, within reason, lies in the development and use of their imagination. We have not yet reached the peak of development in the use of our imaginative capacity. We have only just discovered that we possess imagination and have started using it in a very basic way. We still have much to learn about how to use our imagination effectively. Imagination is a powerful tool that can help us achieve our goals and realize our dreams. By developing and using our imaginative capacity, we can expand our possibilities and achieve great accomplishments. It's important to continue exploring and developing our imagination to make the most of its potential.

Imagination is a powerful faculty that operates in two ways: synthetic imagination and creative imagination.

Synthetic imagination is the ability to rearrange existing concepts, ideas, or plans into new combinations. This faculty does not create anything new but works with the material of experience, education, and observation it receives. It is the faculty most used by inventors, except for "geniuses" who resort to creative imagination when they cannot solve a problem through synthetic imagination.

Creative imagination, on the other hand, is the faculty by which the finite mind of man has direct communication with

Infinite Intelligence. It is through this faculty that we receive "hunches" and "inspirations" and that all new or basic ideas are transmitted to man. It is also through it that an individual can "synchronize" or communicate with the subconscious of others.

Creative imagination works automatically in the manner described on the following pages. This faculty is only activated when the conscious mind works at an accelerated pace, as when it is stimulated by the emotion of a strong desire. The creative faculty becomes more alert as it is developed through use.

To develop creative imagination, it is important to regularly practice activities that stimulate creativity and personal expression. This can include artistic activities such as painting, writing, or music, or visualization and meditation exercises. Additionally, it is important to maintain an open and curious mind, exploring new ideas and perspectives.

Another way to develop creative imagination is through exposure to new experiences and challenges. Travel to unfamiliar places, try new hobbies, or learn a new skill. This will expand your horizons and stimulate your mind to think in new and creative ways.

It is also important to cultivate an environment conducive to creativity. Create a workspace free from distractions, where you can focus on your ideas and projects. Surround yourself with inspiring and motivating people who encourage you to explore your creative potential.

Remember that creative imagination is a faculty that can be developed with practice and dedication. By nurturing your mind with creative and challenging stimuli, you will be strengthening your imaginative capacity and opening the doors to a world of unlimited possibilities.

The impulse of desire for money is powerful, but it's important to remember that you may also face circumstances and situations that require the use of creative imagination. For now, focus on developing synthetic imagination, as it is the faculty you will use most frequently in the process of converting desire into money.

The transformation of the intangible impulse of desire into tangible reality of money requires the use of a plan or plans. These plans must be formulated with the aid of imagination, primarily with the synthetic faculty.

Desire is a thought impulse and thought impulses are forms of energy. When you start with the thought impulse of the desire to accumulate money, you are calling to your service the same "material" that nature used in creating the earth and all material forms of the universe, including the body and brain in which thought impulses operate.

Ideas can be turned into money by the power of defined purpose and defined plans. Wealth comes, if it comes at all, in response to defined demands, based on the application of defined principles and not by chance or luck. Generally, an idea is a thought impulse that impels to action through an appeal to the imagination.

To turn the desire for money into tangible reality, it's important to follow some practical steps. Here are some tips to help you achieve this goal:

Define your purpose: Clearly identify what you want to achieve in financial terms. How much money do you want to accumulate and in what timeframe? Having a defined purpose will give you a sense of direction and motivation to move forward.

Create an action plan: After defining your purpose, create a detailed action plan to achieve it. Identify the necessary steps to reach your financial goal and set realistic deadlines for each stage. This will give you a clear framework to move forward.

Use your imagination: Use your synthetic imagination to create new combinations of ideas and concepts that can help you achieve your financial goal. Additionally, don't be afraid to resort to creative imagination when facing challenges or obstacles.

Track your progress: Regularly monitor your progress towards your financial goal. This will allow you to adjust your action plan as needed and stay focused on your objectives. Additionally, celebrating your achievements along the way will increase your motivation and self-confidence.

Be persistent: Transforming the desire for money into tangible reality requires persistence and determination. Be prepared to face challenges and obstacles along the way, but don't give up. Stay focused on your goals and keep working towards them, step by step.

Andrew Carnegie, J.P. Morgan, Cornelius Vanderbilt, and John D. Rockefeller are examples of men who achieved great financial success by surrounding themselves with talented and creative people. They recognized the importance of having by their side people who knew everything they knew, people who created ideas and put them into action. By doing so, they became fabulously rich.

These men did not wait for favorable "opportunities" to arise. Instead, they created their own opportunities through strategic planning, hard work, and determination. They did not rely on luck but trusted in their abilities and the strength of their teams to achieve success.

The lesson to be learned from these figures is that success rarely comes by chance. It is the result of conscious and consistent effort to achieve defined goals. By surrounding yourself with talented and creative people, setting clear goals, and working hard to achieve them, you too can achieve success in your financial life.

Imagination is a crucial ingredient that is often overlooked on the path to success.

It is the catalyst that transforms ideas into tangible reality. An example of this is Asa Candler, who did not invent the formula for Coca-Cola but provided the imagination necessary to turn it into a fortune.

However, even the most sophisticated tool requires someone who knows how to use it. Everything man creates or acquires begins in the form of desire, and that desire must be fueled by imagination.

To ensure success, it is crucial to have flawless plans. No individual has enough experience, instruction, natural ability, and knowledge to guarantee the accumulation of great wealth without the cooperation of others. Every plan adopted in the effort to accumulate wealth must be a joint creation of yours and all members of your "Master Mind" group. You may originate your own plans, in whole or in part, but have them checked and approved by the members of your "Master Mind" alliance.

Your achievement cannot be greater than the wisdom of your plans. Temporary defeat should mean only one thing: the certainty that there is something wrong with your plans. Millions of men go through life in the greatest poverty and unhappiness because they have no sensible plan for accumulating wealth.

No man is defeated until he gives up in his own mind. When defeat comes, accept it as a sign that your plans are not sound. Rebuild them and sail again toward your desired goal. If you give up before reaching the goal, you will never know what could have been achieved.

It is important to remember that temporary defeat is not a sign of permanent failure. Instead, it is an opportunity to reassess your plans and strategies, identify areas for improvement, and adjust your course of action. By facing defeat with resilience and determination, you will be strengthening your ability to overcome challenges and achieve your goals.

Additionally, it is important to maintain a growth mindset throughout your journey to success. This means being open to new experiences, challenges, and learning opportunities. Challenge yourself to step out of your comfort zone and explore new areas of interest. Set realistic and measurable goals that align with your values and personal aspirations. Track your progress and celebrate your achievements along the way.

Remember that success is a continuous journey, full of ups and downs. Be prepared to face challenges and obstacles along the way, but do not give up. Stay focused on your goals and keep working toward them, step by step. With determination, resilience, and imagination, you can turn your desires into tangible reality.

Nikola Tesla faced temporary defeats not only at the beginning of his career but also after achieving great success. However, he did not give up. Instead, he created new plans and moved forward, achieving financial victory.

A successful leader must plan their work and work their plan. The leader who acts by guesswork, without practical and defined plans, is comparable to a ship without a rudder. Sooner or later, it will end up crashing against the rocks.

No relaxed or careless person can become a successful leader. Leadership demands respect, and followers will not respect a leader who does not have the characteristics of a pleasant personality.

The successful leader must understand and apply the principle of cooperative effort and be able to induce their followers to do the same. Leadership requires power, and power requires cooperation.

Let nothing distract you and be the leader of your own soul. There are two forms of leadership: the first, which is the most efficient, is leadership by consent and with the sympathy of the followers. The second is leadership by force, without the consent and sympathy of the followers.

Leadership by consent is based on the trust, respect, and admiration of the followers for the leader. It is a form of leadership that inspires and motivates people to give their best for a common goal. On the other hand, leadership by force is based on fear and coercion and can generate resentment and resistance from the followers.

To be an effective leader, it is important to seek the consent and sympathy of the followers. This can be achieved through clear communication, the establishment of shared goals, and the demonstration of integrity and competence. By leading by example and inspiring confidence, you will be building a solid foundation for success.

In addition to seeking the consent and sympathy of the followers, there are other strategies that can help you become an effective leader. Here are some additional tips:

Communicate clearly: Communicate your expectations, goals, and vision clearly and concisely. This will help your followers understand what is expected of them and how they can contribute to the team's success.

Listen actively: Actively listen to the opinions, ideas, and concerns of your followers. This will demonstrate that you value their contributions and are willing to consider their perspectives.

Be a role model: Leading by example is one of the most effective ways to inspire confidence and respect in your followers. Demonstrate integrity, competence, and commitment in your actions, and your followers will follow your example.

Recognize and reward: Recognize and reward the good performance of your followers. This will increase their motivation and commitment to the team's success.

Develop your team: Invest in the development of your team by providing learning and growth opportunities. This will help your followers expand their skills and contribute even more to the team's success.

By following these additional tips, you will be developing effective leadership skills that will help you achieve success in your personal and professional journey.

CHAPTER 11.

EXPLORING THE CHARACTERISTICS OF SOME GREAT LEADERS

In studying the great leaders of history, such as Abraham Lincoln, Winston Churchill, Napoleon Bonaparte, Margaret Thatcher, and many others, we analyze the reasons behind their remarkable success. Each of these leaders embodied distinct characteristics and strategies that were fundamental to achieving their goals.

A striking quality of truly great leaders is their willingness to do any kind of work they would ask of others. They deeply understand and respect the truth that "the greatest among you will be the servant of all."

In the world, reward is not based solely on the knowledge one possesses, but rather on the actions taken and the ability to inspire others. An efficient leader, through their knowledge of their position and their magnetic personality, has the power to significantly increase the efficiency of others. They motivate them to offer superior services, far beyond what they could do for themselves without their guidance.

Abraham Lincoln, known for his perseverance and leadership skills, overcame adversities and united a divided nation during the American Civil War. His tireless determination and effective communication skills were fundamental to inspiring the people and promoting change. He faced a nation divided by war and slavery. His relentless pursuit of national unity and equality for all citizens was an example of transformative leadership. He did not give up in the face of difficulties but continued to fight for his ideals until achieving victory.

Winston Churchill, a charismatic leader, was an icon of resistance during World War II. His unwavering courage, oratory skills, and strategic ability allowed him to lead Britain in times of crisis and maintain hope even in the darkest moments. During World War II, he faced one of the most serious threats the world has ever seen. His unwavering courage and confidence in victory inspired not only the British but also people around the world. He refused to succumb to despair, even when defeat seemed imminent, and his determination was crucial to British resistance and the eventual triumph of the Allies.

Napoleon Bonaparte, a brilliant military strategist, conquered much of Europe in a short period. His audacious vision, tactical skills, and ability to inspire his soldiers contributed to his impressive success as a leader and commander. With his strategic and military mind, he was able to conquer extensive territories and establish his empire. His bold vision, coupled with brilliant tactical skills, allowed him to overcome seemingly insurmountable challenges. He knew how to seize opportunities and get the best out of his troops, establishing himself as one of the greatest military leaders in history.

Margaret Thatcher, the first woman to become Prime Minister of the United Kingdom, was known as the "Iron Lady." Her determination, tenacity, and firm stance were instrumental in implementing significant economic and political reforms during her tenure, and she became a symbol of strong and unwavering leadership. A woman in a male-dominated field, she faced significant obstacles and resistance. However, her relentless determination and conviction in the policies she advocated allowed her to implement fundamental economic and political reforms for the United Kingdom. She refused to be discouraged by criticism and persevered in pursuing her goals.

These leaders teach us that success is not the result only of talent or luck, but rather of a set of personal characteristics and developed skills. They show us that resilience, determination, and adaptability are essential for overcoming challenges and achieving lasting success.

Additionally, these leaders also possessed exceptional communication skills. They knew how to articulate their visions, inspire those around them, and build coalitions to achieve common goals. Their rhetorical skills and persuasive abilities enabled them to gain the support and trust of their teams and followers.

Another fundamental aspect of the success of these leaders was their strategic vision. They had a clear understanding of their objectives and developed comprehensive action plans to achieve them. They anticipated challenges, identified opportunities, and made bold decisions while always keeping their focus on their ultimate goals.

Furthermore, they demonstrated transformative leadership skills, meaning they were able to shape the course of history and leave a lasting legacy. They were visionaries who challenged existing norms, promoted significant changes, and made a lasting impact in their respective fields.

The truly great leader does not seek honors for themselves. They are content to see them, if any, being attributed to their followers, for they understand that most will work with greater dedication in pursuit of praise and recognition than simply for money.

A leader who is not loyal to those who trusted in them, to their colleagues, superiors, and subordinates, will not be able to maintain their leadership for long. Disloyalty marks a person as of little value, lower than the dust of the earth, and attracts the contempt they deserve. Lack of loyalty is one of the main causes of failure in all areas of life.

The office door of the true leader is open to all who wish to enter, and their work environment is not marked by formality or ostentation.

CHAPTER 12.

BECOMING THE MASTER OF YOURSELF: DISCIPLINE, ORGANIZATION, AND SELF-MASTERY TO ACHIEVE SUCCESS

Discipline and organization are achieved through self-control, which requires controlling all negative qualities. Before being able to control external circumstances, it is necessary to control oneself. Self-mastery is the most challenging task you will face. If you do not conquer yourself, you will be defeated by yourself. When you look in the mirror, you may simultaneously see your best friend and your worst enemy.

Discipline requires setting clear goals and creating consistent habits to achieve them. Organization involves careful planning, efficient time and space management, and the ability to prioritize tasks.

Remember that discipline and organization are not just about controlling negative aspects but also about cultivating positive qualities. It is necessary to nurture perseverance, motivation, and self-determination to face challenges and persist in your goals.

As you strive to master yourself, you will learn to find balance and harmony in all areas of your life. You will be able to make conscious decisions and align your actions with your values and purposes. Self-mastery is a challenging journey, but the results are rewarding.

Therefore, continue practicing discipline and organization in your daily life. Be willing to confront your own limits and overcome them. Stay committed to your goals and constantly seek personal growth. With perseverance and determination, you will achieve significant progress and become the best version of yourself.

During your journey here on Earth, it is important to avoid unfavorable influences from the environment. As the proverb says, "As the branch bends, so bends the tree." Many people with criminal tendencies develop these inclinations due to the harmful environment and inappropriate friendships throughout life.

It is essential to be aware of the environment you are in and the people you associate with. The environment can exert a significant influence on your thoughts, attitudes, and behaviors. Therefore, seek to surround yourself with positive people who share your values and encourage you to follow a virtuous path.

Stay vigilant against negative influences that may arise in your path. Be selective in choosing your friendships and avoid situations that may compromise your principles and goals. Remember that every choice you make shapes your future, and it is essential that these choices are guided by wisdom and discernment.

By distancing yourself from unfavorable influences, you will create an environment conducive to your personal and moral growth. In this way, you can focus on developing your best qualities and pursuing a fulfilling and meaningful life.

Therefore, be mindful of environmental influences and make conscious choices. Remember that you have the power to shape your own destiny and build a life based on solid and positive principles.

In the Bible, we find the example of Joseph, the son of Jacob. Joseph was sold as a slave by his own brothers and was later taken to Egypt, where he faced a series of challenges and temptations. However, he remained faithful to his principles and resisted the adverse influences of the environment he was in.

A notable example is when Joseph was tempted by Potiphar's wife, an Egyptian officer. She repeatedly pressured him to engage in an illicit relationship, but Joseph remained firm in his moral integrity, refusing to yield to temptations. He said, "How then could I do such a wicked thing and sin against God?" (Genesis 39:9).

Even in the face of difficulties and the pressure of the environment, Joseph chose to act according to his principles and values. His determination to resist unfavorable influences not only protected him from committing a moral mistake but also led him to be exalted and occupy a prominent position in Egypt.

Joseph's example teaches us the importance of remaining faithful to our principles, even when confronted with adverse influences. He shows us that regardless of the circumstances, we can make the right decisions and resist temptations if we stand firm in our convictions.

Like Joseph, it is crucial to be aware of the influences around us and strive to resist the temptations that may compromise our moral integrity. By doing so, we will build strong character and move closer to a life based on solid principles and in accordance with what we believe is right.

Another notable example is that of Daniel, who was taken captive to Babylon along with many other Hebrew youths. In the court of King Nebuchadnezzar, Daniel and his friends were exposed to an environment filled with idolatry and practices contrary to their faith. However, they remained steadfast in their convictions, refusing to participate in pagan rituals and to compromise their worship of the true God.

Despite the pressure and threats, Daniel continued to pray and seek God's guidance. His faithfulness and wisdom were recognized by the king, who elevated him to a position of leadership. Daniel remained upright and resisted adverse influences throughout his life, even when it put him in danger.

This example teaches us that, regardless of the circumstances we find ourselves in, we can choose to follow a path of righteousness and fidelity. We can face unfavorable influences from the environment and resist the pressures that try to lead us away from our values and principles.

By drawing inspiration from the examples in the Bible, such as those of Joseph and Daniel, we can strengthen our determination to remain faithful to our beliefs and resist negative influences that may arise around us. By clinging to our faith, seeking divine guidance, and surrounding ourselves with people who share our values, we can overcome adversity and tread a path of integrity and spiritual fulfillment.

CHAPTER 13.

LIFE AND WISDOM: PROCRASTINATION AND BRAVE BEGINNINGS

Procrastination is a persistent shadow that accompanies the journey of every human being, patiently waiting for the right moment to undermine their chances of success. It is one of the most common causes of failure, leading many to traverse life in the condition of failures. After all, how many of us wait for the elusive "perfect moment" to start something worthwhile?

However, it is important to understand that the ideal moment will never come. It is an illusion that prevents us from moving forward and achieving our goals. Life demands courage and determination to start where we are, using the tools we have at hand.

Wisdom teaches us that we should not passively wait for ideal conditions to act. Instead, we should begin our journey, even if only with modest resources. For as we progress, better tools and opportunities will arise along the way.

The true key to success lies in understanding that life is a continuous journey, full of learning and growth. By taking the first step, we are moving towards our goals and making room for wisdom and opportunities to manifest.

So, do not indefinitely wait for the "exact moment." Instead, embrace life and wisdom by boldly starting your journey, using the resources and skills you possess. As you progress, you will be graced with even better tools, revealing yourself as a wise and victorious protagonist of your own story.

Life is a constant flow of experiences and challenges, in which wisdom plays a fundamental role. By freeing ourselves from the trap of procrastination and starting to act, even with limited resources, we are taking control of our own legacy.

Wisdom teaches us that true greatness lies not in passive waiting, but in the determination to act in the present. Each step taken is an opportunity for learning and growth, and even the simplest tools can prove to be valuable allies along the way.

As we move forward with courage and confidence, wisdom guides us beyond our comfort zone, allowing us to explore new horizons and expand our limits. It shows us that life is a continuous process of discovery, in which opportunities reveal themselves to those willing to take the first step.

Do not worry about the obstacles that may arise along the way. Wisdom teaches us to face them with resilience and perseverance. Each challenge overcome is an opportunity for growth and strengthening, empowering us to deal with future adversities more effectively.

Therefore, free yourself from the illusion of the perfect moment and embrace the wisdom that resides within you. Start where you are, with what you have, and allow yourself to grow and evolve along the way. Life is a journey full of possibilities, and by acting wisely, you will be sailing towards success and personal fulfillment.

A great genius of the last century who embodies wisdom and courageous action is Albert Einstein. Einstein revolutionized our understanding of the universe with his theory of relativity, but his journey was not only marked by brilliant scientific discoveries.

Einstein did not wait for perfect conditions to pursue his passion for physics. He began his career humbly, working as a patent clerk while continuing to explore the mysteries of the universe on his own. He used the tools available to him at the time, his sharp mind, and his insatiable curiosity.

Throughout his life, Einstein faced numerous challenges and obstacles. However, his determination and perseverance were unwavering. He believed that wisdom came from action, and that it took courage to challenge conventions and move forward, even without guarantees of immediate success.

Einstein also understood the importance of learning from failures and adapting to constantly changing circumstances. He did not allow himself to be paralyzed by procrastination or waiting for the perfect moment. Instead, he dove headfirst into his studies and experiments, always seeking new ways to understand the world around him.

His determination and relentless pursuit of knowledge led him to become one of the brightest minds in history. Einstein taught us that life is a journey of discovery and continuous learning, and that wisdom is intrinsically linked to courageous action and perseverance.

Therefore, take inspiration from Einstein's example and do not wait for the perfect moment. Start where you are, with the tools you have at hand, and allow wisdom and opportunities to reveal themselves along your journey. Be brave, persistent, and never let procrastination rob you of your chances of achieving success and fulfillment.

We live in a constantly changing world, where new technologies, trends, and challenges emerge rapidly. In this scenario, the ability to adapt and adjust to circumstances is essential for personal and professional success.

By developing adaptability, you become more flexible and resilient in the face of change. This involves being open to learning new things, abandoning old habits that are no longer relevant, and embracing new ways of thinking and acting.

One way to develop this skill is to constantly seek opportunities for learning and growth. Be willing to explore new areas of knowledge, acquire new skills, and reinvent yourself when necessary. This may involve taking courses, attending workshops, reading books, participating in events, and even having conversations with people who have different perspectives from yours.

Additionally, it is essential to adopt an open and positive mindset towards change. Instead of resisting it, see it as an opportunity to adapt and grow. Be willing to step out of your comfort zone and try new things, even if it may seem challenging at first.

Remember that adaptability is a skill that can be honed over time. The more you expose yourself to different situations and challenges, the more prepared you will be to deal with the uncertainties and changes of the present.

Therefore, constantly seek to develop your adaptability skill. Be open to learning, be flexible in the face of change, and see each challenge as an opportunity to grow and develop. By doing so, you will be prepared to effectively face the challenges of today and seize the opportunities that come your way.

Lack of persistence: It is common to be good at starting projects but struggle to see them through to the end. It is important to develop the ability to persist and finish what we start.

Negative personality: A negative personality can drive people away and hinder success. It is important to cultivate a positive and constructive attitude to attract opportunities and healthy relationships. Those who carry a negative attitude, pushing others away, will not find hope for success.

CHAPTER 14.

CHALLENGING LIMITS: THE ART OF RISKING AND THRIVING IN LIFE

Those who avoid risk often end up with mere crumbs after others have already satisfied themselves with their choices. Both excessive caution and lack of caution are harmful and should be avoided. Life itself is filled with risks and uncertainties.

However, it's important to find a balance between caution and courage, as both excessive and lack of caution can be detrimental.

Successful people keep an open mind and are not afraid to face challenges. They focus their efforts on a primary goal and work diligently to achieve it. Additionally, they cultivate the habit of thrift, saving a defined percentage of their income to invest in their future.

Enthusiasm is an important quality for success. It's contagious and helps to convince and inspire others. On the other hand, lack of enthusiasm can hinder progress and limit opportunities.

Having an open mindset is crucial for personal and professional growth. Those who close themselves off to their own ideas and beliefs rarely make progress. It's important to be willing to learn, explore new perspectives, and adapt to change.

Lastly, it's important to remember that power gained without one's own effort is not a reliable path to success. Those who inherit wealth or power without having worked for them may not be prepared to handle them responsibly. Rapidly acquired wealth can be more dangerous than poverty. True success is achieved through personal effort, determination, and skill development.

Honesty is a fundamental quality for success. While there may be circumstances where temporary dishonesty is unavoidable, intentional dishonesty is never justifiable. Sooner or later, dishonest actions will be uncovered, and the individual will pay the price with the loss of their reputation and possibly their freedom.

Unfortunately, many people are either indifferent or too lazy to gather facts and reason accurately. Instead, they prefer to act based on opinions formed by assumptions or hasty judgments.

An analysis of men and women who have experienced failure revealed that lack of decision is one of the leading causes of failure. Procrastination, the opposite of decision, is a common enemy that everyone must overcome.

On the other hand, an analysis of people who have accumulated fortunes of over a million dollars showed that they all had the habit of making decisions quickly and changing them slowly, if necessary. In contrast, those who fail to accumulate money have the habit of making decisions slowly and changing them frequently and swiftly.

Therefore, it's important to cultivate honesty and the ability to make decisions quickly and decisively. By gathering facts and reasoning accurately, it's possible to make informed decisions and avoid procrastination. Remember that intentional dishonesty is never justifiable and can lead to long-term negative consequences. By acting with integrity and making conscious decisions, it's possible to achieve success sustainably.

One of the notable qualities of successful men like J.P. Morgan and Vanderbilt was the habit of making quick and definitive decisions, changing them slowly if necessary. In contrast, many people who fail to accumulate enough money for their needs are easily influenced by the opinions of others.

It's important to trust your own mind and make your own decisions. If you share your plans and purposes with others, choose carefully those who are in harmony with your goals. Close friends and relatives, even unintentionally, can hinder you with their opinions or ridicule.

Keep your eyes and ears open and your mouth shut if you want to acquire the habit of immediate decision-making. Those who talk too much miss opportunities to gain useful knowledge and reveal their plans to people who may delight in defeating them out of envy. True wisdom is often perceived through modesty and silence.

Remember that everyone around you is also looking for opportunities to accumulate money. If you freely talk about your plans, you may find that someone has already used them to get ahead of you. Therefore, one of your first decisions should be to keep your mouth shut and your eyes and ears open.

To achieve success, it's important to follow six principles: desire, decision, faith, persistence, the "Master Mind" group, and organized planning. Lack of decision is the main cause of failure. Everyone has opinions, but in the end, it's your opinion that moves your world.

A resolute mind harmonizes with tremendous special power. The great desire for freedom brings freedom; the great desire for wealth brings wealth. Every powerful man stays within his own power.

The Bible offers many teachings on how to make wise decisions and live a full and meaningful life. Proverbs 3:5-6 advises us to trust in God and seek His guidance in all our decisions: "Trust in the Lord with all your heart and lean not on your own understanding; in all your ways submit to him, and he will make your paths straight."

By seeking divine wisdom and trusting in God, we can make decisions aligned with our higher values and purposes. We can also find peace and confidence, knowing that God is with us in all our journeys.

Additionally, the Bible encourages us to seek wisdom through study and reflection. Proverbs 4:7 reminds us of the importance of wisdom: "The beginning of wisdom is this: Get wisdom. Though it cost all you have, get understanding." By studying the Scriptures and seeking knowledge, we can develop a deeper understanding of the world and make wiser decisions.

Therefore, when making important decisions, it's important to seek divine guidance and trust in God. It's also important to study the Scriptures and seek wisdom through continuous learning. By doing so, we can make decisions aligned with our highest values and live a full and meaningful life.

Many men who accumulate great fortunes are seen as cold and cruel, but this is not always true. They have a quality that sets them apart from others: persistence. This word may not sound heroic, but it is essential for success. Persistence is like the coal that hardens the steel of character.

Fortunes are not the result of chance but of preparing the mind to attract them. The subconscious works day and night to fulfill our desires. But without persistence, nothing is achieved. Persistence is the key to overcoming obstacles and defeats. Those who are persistent never give up and reach the top of the ladder of wealth.

Persistence is not a gift but a habit that can be learned and cultivated. For this, it's necessary to have some factors:

Defined purpose: knowing what you want is the first step to developing persistence. A clear goal motivates us to overcome difficulties.

Desire: the more intense our desire, the easier it is to maintain persistence. Desire is the fuel of action.

Self-confidence: believing in yourself and your ability to execute a plan makes us persist until the end. Self-confidence can be strengthened by the principle described in the chapter on success.

Defined plans: having organized and written plans helps us to focus and direct ourselves. Plans should be based on precise knowledge and not on assumptions.

Cooperation: relying on the support and understanding of others encourages us to persist. Cooperation is the strength of unity.

Willpower: the habit of focusing thought on forming plans to achieve defined purposes leads us to persistence. Willpower is the discipline of the mind.

Persistence is the fruit of habit. The mind is shaped by the experiences we live daily. Fear, the worst enemy of persistence, can be overcome by the repetition of acts of courage. Those who have faced a war know this.

Success depends on making organized plans, in writing, where they can be analyzed.

Many people fail to live their own lives for fear of criticism from relatives, in the name of duty. But duty does not mean sacrificing your personal ambitions and your right to choose how you want to live.

People also shy away from a big dream or give up a profession for fear of criticism that may arise if they fail. In these cases, fear is stronger than the desire for success.

Some people avoid a big dream or renounce a profession for fear of the opinions of family and "acquaintances," who may say, "Don't be so ambitious, they'll think you're crazy."

The only chance we can count on is the chance created by ourselves.

CHAPTER 15.

MUHAMMAD: THE MIRACLE-LESS PROPHET AND HIS CONTROVERSIAL MESSAGE

Muhammad was a prophet, yet he performed no recognized miracles. He lacked academic training and mystical experience; he only began his mission at the age of forty. When he declared himself the messenger of God, bringing the message of the true religion, he was mocked and called mad. He suffered aggression from children and women, was expelled from his hometown, Mecca, and his followers were stripped of their belongings and sent to the desert to join him. After ten years of preaching, all he had to show for it was exile, poverty, and disdain. However, in less than a decade, he became the lord of Arabia, the governor of Mecca, and the founder of a new world religion, which would spread from Persia to the Iberian Peninsula, propelled by the force he bestowed upon it. This force was threefold: the power of words, the efficacy of prayer, and man's proximity to God. His journey seems inexplicable.

Muhammad was born into a noble but impoverished family in Mecca. Mecca was a commercial and religious center, home to the sacred stone called the Kaaba, which housed 360 idols. For hygienic reasons, the children of Mecca were raised in the desert by the Bedouins. Muhammad also underwent this experience, drinking the milk of nomadic mothers and tending to sheep. Later, he was hired by a wealthy widow as the head of her caravans. He traveled throughout the East, conversing with many men of different beliefs, observing the decline of Christianity into conflicting sects. At the age of twenty-eight, he married the widow Khadija, who seduced him and deceived his father to obtain his blessing. For twelve years, Muhammad lived as a wealthy, respected, and astute merchant. Then, he began to withdraw to the desert and returned one day with the first verse of the Quran, telling Khadija that the angel Gabriel had appeared to him, commanding him to be the messenger of God. The Quran was the word revealed by God and was the closest thing to a miracle in Muhammad's life. He had never been a poet nor had eloquence. Yet, the verses of the Quran, when received and recited to the faithful, surpassed the verses produced by the professional poets of the tribes. To the Arabs, this was a miracle. For them, the gift of speech was the greatest gift, and the poet was all-powerful. Furthermore, the Quran taught that all men were equal before God and that the world should be a democratic state - Islam. It was this political heresy, along with Muhammad's desire to destroy the 360 idols in the courtyard of the Kaaba, that led to his banishment. The idols attracted desert tribes to Mecca, generating profits. Therefore, the merchants of Mecca, the capitalists of whom Muhammad had been a part, turned against him. He took refuge in the desert and proclaimed his sovereignty over the world.

    We can compare the story of Muhammad with the stories of other prophets or geniuses of the past century who faced similar difficulties in conveying their messages or ideas. For example: Moses was a prophet who liberated the Israelites from slavery in Egypt and revealed divine law to them at Mount Sinai. He also performed various miracles before Pharaoh and his people, such as turning his staff into a serpent, parting the Red Sea, and bringing forth water from a rock. However, he also faced opposition and disbelief from some Israelites, who worshipped a golden calf while he was on the mountain and murmured against him in the desert. Moses had to endure the rebellion and ingratitude of his people for forty years until he led them to the borders of the Promised Land. (Exodus 1-20; Numbers 11-14; Deuteronomy 34)

    Gandhi was a political and spiritual leader who fought for India's independence from British rule and for nonviolence as a form of resistance. He also advocated for the rights of untouchables, religious minorities, and women in Indian society. He inspired millions of Indians to follow his principles of satyagraha (adherence to truth) and ahimsa (non-injury). However, he also faced hostility and violence from some radical groups, who accused him of being pro-Muslim or anti-Hindu. He was imprisoned several times by the British, suffered physical and verbal attacks, and was assassinated by a Hindu fanatic in 1948. (Gandhi: A Biography, by Geoffrey Ashe)

Einstein was a scientific genius who revolutionized physics with his theories of relativity and quantum mechanics. He also contributed to the understanding of the universe, matter, and energy. He received the Nobel Prize in Physics in 1921 and was recognized as one of the greatest thinkers in history. However, he also faced difficulties and persecution because of his Jewish background and pacifist ideas. He had to flee Nazi Germany in 1933, saw his theory of relativity being banned and his books burned by the Nazis, and was monitored by the FBI in the United States on suspicion of being a communist. He also opposed the use of the atomic bomb, which was based on his discovery of the equivalence between mass and energy.

Persistence shapes character like carbon transforms brittle iron into resilient steel. With persistence, you will develop a magical sense of prosperity, while the subconscious is in constant action to bring you the money you desire.

People like Fannie Hurst, Kate Smith, W. C. Fields teach us the value of persistence. Muhammad and others show us how persistence changes the course of history. Four simple steps create the habit of persistence, overcoming any negative or discouraging influences that may have affected you so far.

Andrew Carnegie's Secret of Success "the union of knowledge and effort, in a climate of harmony, between two or more people, to achieve a defined goal." No individual can wield great power without understanding the law of attraction and the law of vibration.

Carnegie's group consisted of a team of nearly fifty men, with whom he associated, with the defined goal of producing and selling steel. He credited all his fortune to the power he had accumulated through this "Mind."

Analyze the results of anyone who has accumulated great wealth and many who have accumulated modest fortunes, and you will see that, consciously or unconsciously, no other principle can generate such great power! You May Need More Intelligence than You Have The human brain can be compared to an electric battery. It is a known fact that a set of batteries will provide more energy than a single battery. It is also known that an individual battery will provide energy in proportion to the number and capacity of the cells it possesses. The brain works in a similar way. Hence the fact that some brains are more efficient than others, which leads us to an important statement: a set of coordinated (or connected) brains, in a spirit of harmony, provide more thought energy than a single brain, just as a set of electric batteries provide more energy than a single battery.

The secret of power lies in men who join other intelligent men. Thus, they can better understand the psychic phase of the law of attraction: when a group of individual minds coordinates and harmonizes, the increased energy generated by this union is available to any individual mind in the group. It is a known fact that Henry Ford began his business career facing the difficulties of poverty, illiteracy, and ignorance. It is also a known fact that, in just ten years, Ford overcame these three difficulties and that, in twenty-five years, he became one of the richest men in the United States.

Money is elusive and cunning. It must be attracted and conquered by methods similar to those used by a suitor determined to charm his preferred lady. And, by chance, the power used to "attract" money is not so different from that used to attract a maiden. This power, if successfully used in the pursuit of money, must be imbued with faith. It must be imbued with desire. It must be imbued with persistence. It must be applied through a plan, and that plan must be put into practice. When money comes in abundance, it flows to those who accumulate it as easily as water flows down a mountain.

The positive emotions of thought form the favorable side that leads to fortune. Negative emotions form the unfavorable side that leads to poverty.

The human mind is a form of energy. When two or more minds cooperate in harmony, they form a great "reservoir" of energy, as well as a third invisible force, comparable to the Higher Mind. Planning and organizing are necessary to become rich. Remaining poor is very easy; poverty requires no plans.

A better definition of genius is the "man who has learned to increase the intensity of thought to the point of being able to communicate freely with sources of knowledge beyond the reach of ordinary thought."

The existence of the sixth sense, which is creative imagination, has been reasonably proven. However, most people do not utilize this ability throughout their lives, and when they do, it is usually by chance. Few people intentionally and purposefully use the capacity of creative imagination with a planned purpose. Those who do so voluntarily, fully understanding their functions, are considered geniuses. The "sixth sense" is the ability that sets geniuses apart from the common individual.

What is commonly referred to as "consciousness" operates entirely through the capacity of the sixth sense.

Those who possess the ability to consciously and deliberately use the sixth sense, fully exploring creative imagination, are capable of achieving extraordinary feats. By understanding and mastering this ability, they stand out as geniuses in their respective fields.

While most people underutilize or neglect the potential of the sixth sense, geniuses recognize its importance and actively cultivate it. They understand that creative imagination is an endless source of innovative ideas, creative solutions, and unique visions.

These ingenious individuals are able to visualize possibilities beyond the reach of most, giving them a significant advantage in their achievements.

The sixth sense is a powerful instrument that permeates the mind of the genius, allowing them to grasp profound insights, connect seemingly disparate ideas, and anticipate future trends. They use this ability to pave new paths, revolutionize fields of knowledge, and leave a lasting legacy.

Therefore, recognizing and developing the sixth sense is crucial to unlocking the creative potential within each of us. The more we dedicate ourselves to exploring and nurturing this unique sense, the closer we will be to uncovering our own genius and making meaningful contributions to the world around us.

There is a great speaker who only achieves greatness when he closes his eyes and begins to rely entirely on the capacity of creative imagination. When asked why he closes his eyes well before reaching the peak of his oratory, he replied: "I do it because then I speak through ideas that come from within." One of America's most successful and famous financiers had the habit of closing his eyes for two or three minutes before making a decision. When asked why he did it, he replied: "With closed eyes, I can draw inspiration from a source of higher intelligence."

The human mind reacts to stimuli! Among the greatest, most powerful stimuli is sexual impulse. When controlled and transformed, this overwhelming force is capable of elevating men to the highest sphere of thought, enabling them to overcome the sources of insignificant worries and annoyances that block their path on the lower plane.

Sexual energy is the creative energy of all geniuses. There has never been, nor will there ever be, a great leader, builder, or artist who did not have the driving force of sex. Surely no one will misinterpret these statements, understanding that all sexually strong individuals are geniuses. A man only reaches the status of genius when and if he stimulates his mind in such a way as to gather the forces at his disposal through the creative capacity of imagination. The primary among the stimuli capable of producing this "breakthrough" is sexual energy. The mere possession of energy is not sufficient to produce genius. Energy must be transformed from a desire for physical contact into another form of desire and action, before elevating someone to the capacity of genius. Far from becoming geniuses through great sexual desire, most men degrade themselves, through ignorance and misuse of this great force, to the status of lower animals.

Based on the analysis of more than twenty-five thousand people, it has been concluded that men who achieve notable success usually do not reach it before the age of forty. More often, it is only after they surpass fifty years old that they truly hit their stride and achieve significant results.

This finding suggests that notable success often results from a life journey filled with experiences, learning, and personal development over the years. However, it is important to emphasize that each person has their own path to success, and this conclusion is based on a statistical analysis of a large number of cases. There are individuals who achieve notable success at younger ages, as well as others who reach it at different times throughout their lives.

Regardless of the age at which notable success is achieved, it is valuable to recognize the importance of continuous learning, perseverance, and dedication to reaching meaningful goals. Time and experience can play a fundamental role in the journey toward success, allowing individuals to develop their skills and knowledge more comprehensively before reaching their professional peak.

One of the main reasons for failure is the lack of control over sexual desire. When uncontrolled, sexual energy can make men impulsive, irrational, and emotional. They lose the ability to think clearly and to plan their actions. Moreover, they also lose connection with God, who is the source of all wisdom and power.

On the other hand, when sexual energy is controlled and transformed, it becomes a powerful force for good. It stimulates the mind to create original ideas and to solve problems. It also connects the mind with God, who is the creator of all things. Sexual energy, when used correctly, is the sixth sense that allows man to communicate with God and to receive His guidance and inspiration.

However, there is still hope for those who realize the value of their energies and seek to channel them in a more constructive way. By adopting greater self-awareness and emotional management, it is possible to redirect powerful emotions to promote healthy relationships, personal growth, and significant contributions to society. Through reflection, continuous learning, and the establishment of clear goals, one can transform dissipation into lasting achievements and a life full of purpose.

The desire for sexual expression is undoubtedly the strongest and most compulsive human emotion. For this reason, when controlled and transmuted into action other than physical expression, it can lead to great accomplishments. You now have the knowledge to create the most magnificent version of yourself. This version already exists in the frequency of the "most magnificent version of you." Decide what you want to be, do, and have, think about it, emit the frequency, and your vision will become your life.

A simple handshake or touch of the hand instantly indicates the presence or absence of magnetism.

CHAPTER 16.

THE POWER OF FAITH AND THE SUBCONSCIOUS

A brief question: What was the best year of your life?

It rarely begins with a salary increase. It's not about money, it's about highly creative effort in any field of activity before the age of forty. The average man reaches the period of greatest creative capacity and success between the ages of forty and sixty. These statements are based on the analysis of thousands of men and women subjected to careful observation. They should serve as encouragement for those who achieve nothing before the age of forty and for those who fear approaching "old age" around forty. Between forty and fifty are usually the most fertile years. Man should approach this age not with fear and trembling, but with hope and eager anticipation.

If you want proof that most men do not begin their best work before forty, study the achievements of the most successful men in the United States and you will find them. Remember that Henry Ford only achieved fulfillment after forty. Andrew Carnegie was well past forty when he began to reap the rewards of his efforts. James Hill, at forty, was still operating the telegraph. His stupendous achievements only took place after that age. Biographies of American industrialists and financiers are filled with evidence that the period from forty to sixty is the most productive age of man.

Between thirty and forty, man begins to learn (if he ever does) about the SUBCONSCIOUS, which is constituted by a field of consciousness where every impulse of thought that reaches the conscious mind through any of the five senses is classified and filed, and can be consulted or withdrawn like cards from a file. The subconscious receives and archives sensory impressions or thoughts of any nature. You can voluntarily plant in your subconscious any plan, thought, or purpose that you wish to translate into its physical or monetary equivalent. The subconscious acts first on dominant desires mixed with emotional feelings, such as faith.

The subconscious works day and night. By a method unknown to man, the subconscious draws strength from Infinite Intelligence to have the power with which it voluntarily transmutes desires into their physical equivalent, always using the most practical means to achieve this objective.

Impulses of thought, both negative and positive, are continually reaching the subconscious. The energy of the whole universe can assist your prayers to be answered. Man is as great as the measure of his thought.

CHAPTER 17.

THE BRAIN AND CONSCIOUSNESS

The human brain is a transmitting and receiving station for thought vibrations, working 24 hours a day to connect its networks of neurons. It has been determined that there are between ten and fourteen billion nerve cells in the human cerebral cortex, organized in defined patterns. These organizations are not random, but ordered. Recently developed methods of electrophysiology allow the deactivation of streams of cells or fibers located with precision using microelectrodes, amplifying them with radio tubes, and recording potential differences of up to one millionth of a volt.

Creative imagination is the "receiving apparatus" of the brain that receives thoughts emitted by other brains. It is the communication agency between the conscious or rational mind and the four sources from which thought stimuli are received. Through emotions, thought vibrations can be increased.

The subconscious is the "transmitting station" of the brain, through which thought vibrations are emitted. Creative imagination is the "receiving apparatus" that captures thought energies. Along with the important factors of the subconscious and the faculty of creative imagination, which constitute the transmitter and receiver apparatus of your mental machine, consider now the principle of auto-suggestion, which is the means by which you can put the "transmitting station" into operation.

The operation of your mental "transmitting station" is a relatively simple process. Just keep in mind three principles and apply them when you want to use the transmitting station: the subconscious, creative imagination, and auto-suggestion. The stimuli by which you put these three principles into action have been described - and the process begins with desire.

Would it not be likely that the same system that provides billions of brain cells with the means of communication with each other also provides the means of communication with other minds?

The central nervous system is incredibly complex, and there is still much to be discovered about how it functions. However, we know that it plays a fundamental role in how we think, feel, and act. By better understanding how the central nervous system works, we can learn to control our thoughts and emotions and achieve our goals.

My goal in allowing my imagination to manifest during these nighttime encounters was clear: to transform my character to represent a combination of the traits of my imaginary mentors. I selected a few mentors who left an extraordinary legacy for humanity, mentioned some previously, and will now reinforce some names like Emerson, Edison, Darwin, Lincoln, Popper, John D. Rockefeller, JP Morgan, and Carnegie. However, it is widely considered, including by my opinion and that of many, that the most remarkable of all was and still is Jesus, with whom I establish daily connection. Almost every night, or during the silence of the early morning hours, I seek a moment alone with God, in search of guidance and advice.

With each encounter, I acquired deeper knowledge of the principles of organized effort they used so effectively.

The starting point of all achievement is desire. The end point is the kind of knowledge that leads to understanding - understanding of oneself, understanding of others, understanding of the laws of nature, and recognition of happiness.

Work on procrastination and avoid the habit of postponing until tomorrow what should have been done today. Stop making excuses and blaming others for everything that goes wrong around you. Stay focused on your goal. Procrastination is closely linked to excessive caution, doubt, and worry; refusal to accept responsibilities and a willingness to avoid commitments. Keep fighting firmly; accept difficulties and stop taking unnecessary shortcuts.

Move forward and give more to receive the blessings that God has for you. Do not demand prosperity and wealth, contentment, and happiness; just avoid failure. But if it happens, keep going and break the barrier. Fall seven times and get up eight. Give thanks, pray, and have intimacy with God. Give thanks more times a day.

Instead of burning bridges and making crossing impossible, create a strategy. Listen more and speak less - that's why we have two ears and one mouth. Have self-confidence and a defined purpose. Exercise self-control, initiative, and enthusiasm. Be ambitious - this is not a sin.

Fear nothing, for you are a descendant of the holder of wealth and power, the one who granted you wisdom and blesses you daily. Throughout life, we face various problems that can be solved more quickly or may take longer. Many had a disturbing childhood with ignorant parents due to their own ancestral origin. Do not blame them and avoid criticizing them. Physical or psychological aggression toward a child can lead to chaos, an irreversible disaster. We need to keep our minds active, we must donate and have compassion. Avoid toxic friendships, as many people are cruel, lost, avoid thinking, and are lazy to reason.

Many suffer from mental inertia, unable to reason properly. About 98% of the world's population is stuck in a comfort zone, like a 'barrel of waste', unwilling to leave because of laziness. Only 2% or less live in a different dimension, being successful in love, belief, understanding, faith, and prosperity.

A wise man, whose wisdom transcends this incident, once stated: 'If someone asks me how I am, I will always say that I am well and grateful. This is the law of vibration: if you believe, you will receive'.

Worries, fears, discouragements, and disappointments in love and business feed the seed of failure. Therefore, we must focus on good things, such as cultivating positive thoughts, seeking self-development, and gratitude for the blessings of life. Instead of being carried away by negativity, it is important to direct our energy toward what drives and inspires us.

Those who achieve success in love, belief, understanding, faith, and prosperity are individuals who are willing to leave their comfort zone and face challenges. They invest time and effort in personal improvement, in the search for knowledge, and in building healthy relationships.

Moreover, it is essential to maintain an abundance mindset, believing that there are unlimited opportunities available to everyone. This involves abandoning the scarcity mindset and cutthroat competition, and embracing the idea of cooperation and collaboration.

Each of us has the power to change our reality and transcend the limitations imposed by laziness and inertia. By taking responsibility for our choices and actions, we can free ourselves from the "barrel of waste" and create a life full of meaning and significance.

Therefore, do not allow laziness and complacency to dominate your life. Constantly seek personal growth, maintain a positive mindset, believe in yourself, and be willing to leave your comfort zone. Thus, you will be closer to being part of the 2% who live in another dimension of success and fulfillment.

CHAPTER 18.

DISCOVERING THE STRATEGIC ESSENCE: WHO WE ARE, WHERE WE COME FROM, AND WHERE WE'RE GOING

"Who we are, where we come from, and where we're going" is a question that transcends the boundaries of philosophy and religion, also entering the realm of business. Some of us have understood that exploring this question can be the path to achieving a higher level compared to others.

By deeply understanding our origins and purposes, we are able to chart a clear and strategic course towards a better future. This quest not only allows us to understand our identity and core values but also helps us align our actions and decisions with a long-term vision.

In the context of business, understanding who we are means identifying our competencies, experiences, and unique resources. This enables us to leverage our distinct advantages and develop a solid, differentiated, and attractive value proposition for our customers and partners.

By investigating where we come from, we delve into our history and learn from our past successes and failures. We analyze our mistakes and successes, absorb valuable lessons, and apply this knowledge to make more informed and strategic decisions in the present.

As for the question of where we're going, it invites us to dream and define ambitious and inspiring goals. By establishing a clear vision of the desired future, we can create strategies and action plans that lead us toward that destination. This vision motivates us, fuels our creativity, and helps us overcome obstacles along the way.

Therefore, exploring who we are, where we come from, and where we're going in the context of business is a powerful and transformative approach. Those who dedicate themselves to this quest, with an open mind and determination, have the opportunity to achieve higher levels of success, impact, and fulfillment. It is an invitation to embark on a journey of self-discovery and conquest, towards a future that exceeds expectations with limitless possibilities.

As we delve into this discussion, we open doors to innovation, reinvention, and growth. Understanding our essence and purpose allows us to identify opportunities that align with our values and long-term vision. We can explore new markets, develop innovative products and services, and establish strategic partnerships that drive our business forward.

Furthermore, when we understand who we are and where we're going, we are able to attract and engage people who share our vision and mission. Motivated and engaged collaborators become powerful allies in the pursuit of extraordinary results. Teams aligned with a common purpose have the potential to overcome challenges, face changes, and achieve exceptional levels of performance.

However, this journey is not easy. It requires self-awareness, courage, and perseverance. It is necessary to investigate our limiting beliefs, question our assumptions, and be willing to step out of our comfort zone. It is a continuous process of learning and adaptation, in which we will face obstacles and failures, but also experience achievements and personal and business growth.

The discussion of who we are, where we come from, and where we're going is more than a philosophical or religious question. It is an opportunity to elevate our businesses to a new level, driven by a deep understanding of our identity and purpose. By embracing this journey, we can explore new horizons, surpass limits, and achieve extraordinary results. It is a quest worth undertaking, as it will lead us to a better and more rewarding place than we could ever imagine.

In elementary physics, we learn that neither matter nor energy (the only realities known to man) can be created or destroyed. Both matter and energy can be transformed, but never destroyed. Life is energy, without a doubt. If neither energy nor matter can be destroyed, it is clear that life cannot be destroyed either. Like other forms of energy, it can undergo various processes of transition or transformation, but it cannot be destroyed.

You have the power to control your mind and provide it with the thought impulses you choose. Men who accumulate great wealth always guard against evil, while the destitute never do. Those who succeed in any profession must prepare their minds to resist evil.

To protect yourself against negative influences, whether of your own creation or the result of the activities of negative people around you, recognize that you have willpower and use it constantly until you form a wall of immunity against negative influences in your mind. Recognize the fact that you and all human beings are naturally lazy, indifferent, and susceptible to suggestions that harmonize with your weaknesses.

If you cannot control your mind, rest assured that you will not be able to control anything else. If you must be careless with your possessions, let it be with material things. Your mind is your spiritual property! Protect it and use it wisely.

Human habits have remained the same since ancient times, only manifested differently. A careful analysis has revealed that women tend to be more susceptible to fear than men.

The human race often lacks gratitude and complains incessantly. As you age, it is important to express gratitude for reaching this age, as it is at this stage that wisdom is acquired and the peak of productive consciousness is reached.

It is possible to control the mind and direct thought impulses according to our choice. Men who accumulate great wealth always guard against evil, while the less fortunate often neglect this precaution. Those who achieve success in any profession must prepare their minds to resist negative influences.

To shield yourself from negative influences, whether they are the result of your own creation or from negative individuals surrounding you like hyenas, aspire to be an eagle and embody the strength of a lion. Stand firm in your dreams and reach a level beyond attainable. Stay at the top as a leader and receive divine protection. Accept God's blessing and cultivate your mind through tireless work.

Recognize the natural human tendency toward laziness, indifference, and susceptibility to suggestions aligned with weaknesses. Then, confront these inclinations and overcome them with determination.

If you do not master your mind, prepare yourself to have no control over anything else! And if there is anything you must be negligent about, let it be with material things, not with your precious mind! It is your spiritual property, so protect it and use it with the care that a divine gift truly deserves!

When studying the history of any man who has achieved remarkable success, it will be observed that he has mastery over his mind, directing it toward the attainment of defined goals. He who fears not triumphs in distant horizons. You can accumulate monetary wealth and invaluable riches - although money can help you find happiness, longevity, enjoyment, and peace of mind.

However, it is important to remember that the true value of life goes beyond mere material wealth. Finding satisfaction and fulfillment requires more than accumulating money. It is essential to seek a balance between financial success and other important areas of life, such as relationships, health, and purpose.

At the same time, it is necessary to recognize that money can play a significant role in providing comfort and opportunities. It can facilitate the realization of aspirations, enable access to resources, and allow for enriching experiences.

However, it is crucial not to lose sight of the essential aspects of existence. The pursuit of true happiness and personal fulfillment requires a holistic approach, which values not only financial prosperity but also personal growth, contribution to society, and the creation of meaningful relationships.

Therefore, while pursuing success and accumulating wealth, it is important to remember to cultivate a balanced mindset, valuing not only money but also the intangible aspects of life that bring true meaning and contentment.

CHAPTER 19.

DIRECTING YOUR MIND TOWARDS GROWTH AND PROSPERITY

The key to success lies in mastering your mind and directing your thoughts towards growth and prosperity. It is necessary to develop a positive and empowering mindset, believing that you are capable of achieving great accomplishments.

Do not settle for mediocre results. Explore success stories and learn from those who have already achieved what you desire. Study their strategies, their mindsets, and how they faced challenges.

Remember that financial success is not just about accumulating material wealth but also about having freedom, personal fulfillment, and the ability to make a difference in the lives of others.

Dive headfirst into your financial plan, programming your mind for success. Feed on knowledge, practice self-discipline, and build habits that drive your progress.

Many people work hard but fail to progress. They desire prosperity but are stuck in negative thoughts about success and money.

Do not be afraid. I have never been afraid. Perhaps God is testing your faith. Think big and aim for the stars to hit the moon. Follow the example of prosperous men, study them, and analyze them.

The journey towards success requires consistency and dedication. Cultivate a growth mindset, where every obstacle is seen as an opportunity for learning and personal growth.

Remember that success does not happen overnight. It requires time, effort, and patience. Stay committed to your goals, even when results take time to materialize.

Harness the power of visualization and positive affirmation. Imagine yourself achieving your goals and repeat positive affirmations to strengthen your belief in yourself and the success you are pursuing.

Create an environment conducive to success. Surround yourself with people who share your vision and encourage you to go further. Avoid negative influences and stay focused on your goals.

Learn from mistakes and failures along the way. See them as opportunities for growth and adjust your approach if necessary. Persist in the face of adversity and be willing to adapt and evolve.

Stay updated and open to new ideas and trends. Be willing to step out of your comfort zone and constantly seek self-improvement.

Remember that financial success is just one part of the equation. Strive for a balance between your financial life, health, relationships, and overall well-being.

With determination, self-discipline, and a positive mindset, you are capable of achieving financial success and living the abundant life you desire. Believe in yourself, stay motivated, and never give up on your dreams. The power is in your hands to create the future you deserve.

In the past, I used to get distracted by shiny short-term opportunities or lose interest when things weren't going well. But I realized that my own mind was my biggest obstacle to success.

Believe me, there is no right side without a left side. Just being in the right place at the right time is not enough. You need to become the right person, be in the right place, and at the right time.

Your character, your thoughts, and your beliefs are the factors that determine your level of success. And what is your ability to act despite fear, worry, discomfort? Can you move forward even when you don't feel like it?

Remember, you have incredible internal potential! Awaken it with confidence, self-esteem, and enthusiasm, and you will become unstoppable in the pursuit of success. Your destiny is in your hands, and you are capable of overcoming any challenge that arises in your path. It's time to shine and achieve great accomplishments!

You are an extraordinary human being, endowed with unique abilities and talents. Believe in yourself and in your power of achievement. Do not let fear, worry, or discomfort stop you from moving towards your goals.

Remember that success does not happen by chance. It is the result of a strong mindset, determination, and consistent action. Even when you don't feel motivated, it's important to gather courage and persistence to keep moving forward.

Do not let obstacles or adverse circumstances derail you from your path. See them as opportunities for growth and learning. Your ability to overcome them will strengthen your character and propel your success.

Believe in the power of your beliefs and positive thoughts. Cultivate a mindset of abundance, gratitude, and self-confidence. This mindset will be a magnet for attracting opportunities and opening doors to success.

Remember that you have control over your own life. Take responsibility for your choices and actions. Be proactive, resilient, and determined to achieve your dreams.

So, free yourself from self-imposed limitations. Open yourself to the unlimited potential that exists within you. Success is within your reach, as long as you believe in yourself, maintain positivity, and move forward with determination. You are destined for great achievements!

You are an endless source of energy and enthusiasm. Let your light shine brightly and inspire the world around you. Do not worry about what others think or say, because the true power lies within you.

Face each challenge as an opportunity to grow and surpass yourself. No matter how difficult it may seem, stand firm and confident. Allow yourself to step out of your comfort zone and face the unknown. It is in these moments that real magic happens and you discover what you are truly capable of.

Remember that success is a continuous journey, not a final destination. Celebrate every small victory along the way and use them as fuel to drive your progress. Have patience and persistence, because great things take time to materialize.

Unconditionally believe in yourself and your abilities. You possess all the resources necessary to achieve your dreams. Believe in your ability to create your own reality and manifest your deepest desires.

Nourish your spirit with positive thoughts, powerful affirmations, and vivid visualizations of the success you wish to achieve. Feel the emotion and vibration of these achievements as if they were already real. This positive energy will attract favorable circumstances and amazing opportunities into your life.

So, rise with confidence, embrace your self-esteem, and know that success is within your reach. You are a shining being capable of extraordinary things. Believe in yourself and move forward with courage, passion, and determination.

CHAPTER 20.

AWAKENING YOUR INNER POTENTIAL: THE KEY TO SUCCESS LIES WITHIN YOU!

Believe that the key to success is awakening your own energy and attracting people to you. When they come, seize the opportunities to thrive financially. However, many people lack the mindset and skills needed to accumulate and maintain large amounts of money, making it difficult to face the challenges that success brings. This explains why many people fail to become wealthy.

Have you ever noticed that those who win the lottery often end up losing everything? Research consistently shows that, regardless of the size of the prize, most of these lucky individuals end up returning to their original financial state, meaning they have the amount of money they can handle more easily.

In the case of those who become rich through their own efforts, the opposite happens. Note that when such a millionaire loses their fortune, they usually recover it in a short time. Some multimillionaires have had billions of dollars and lost everything, left with not a penny. But some time later, they regained everything and even got more. Do they have a magnet for money? How is this phenomenon explained? It's simple. They can lose all the money they have, but they never lose the recipe for their success: Never neglect the importance of thought, nurture your mind, stay focused, and strengthen your faith. Here are some tips to help you in your pursuit of financial success:

1. Set clear goals: Establish tangible and measurable financial goals to help guide your efforts. Determine how much money you want to earn, how much you want to save, and what financial

milestones you want to achieve within specific timeframes. This will help maintain focus and motivation along the way.

2. Develop healthy financial habits: Cultivate positive financial practices such as creating a budget, saving regularly, tracking your expenses, avoiding excessive debt, and paying your bills on time. Small consistent actions over time can have a significant impact on your financial health.

3. Diversify your income sources: Consider diversifying your income sources by exploring additional business opportunities or investments. Having multiple income sources can help protect you against financial emergencies and increase your earning potential.

4. Manage risks: Be aware of financial risks and take steps to mitigate them. This may involve creating an emergency fund, obtaining adequate insurance to protect your assets and health, and conducting risk analysis on your investments to make informed decisions.

5. Learn from mistakes: Recognize that making financial mistakes is part of the learning and growth process. Instead of becoming discouraged, view these mistakes as learning opportunities. Analyze what went wrong, adapt your approach, and move forward with greater wisdom.

6. Seek professional guidance: If necessary, consider working with a financial advisor or investment specialist. They can offer specialized insight, help create customized strategies, and provide guidance to maximize your chances of financial success.

7. Seize learning opportunities: Be open to learning from others and their experiences. Attend workshops, seminars, and conferences on personal finance and investments. Additionally, take advantage of online resources such as articles, blogs, and educational videos to expand your financial knowledge.

8. Stay updated on the financial market: Be aware of trends and changes in the financial market. Follow economic news, read reports, and stay informed about developments in the sectors you

are interested in. This will help you make informed decisions when investing and managing your money.

9. Be willing to make "sacrifices": Financial success often requires sacrifices and discipline. Be willing to give up unnecessary expenses, make conscious choices, and adopt a lifestyle that aligns with your financial goals. Remember that small sacrifices today can lead to great rewards in the future.

10. Make adjustments as needed: As you progress toward your financial goals and success, be willing to reassess and adjust your strategy as needed. Personal and economic circumstances may change over time, so be open to making adjustments to adapt to new realities.

11. Cultivate an abundance mindset: Instead of focusing on scarcity, cultivate an abundance mindset and gratitude. Believe that there are unlimited financial opportunities available and be open to receiving them. Gratitude helps maintain a positive perspective, even during financial challenges.

12. Do not compare yourself to others: Financial success is personal and unique to each individual. Avoid comparing your financial journey to that of others, as this can lead to feelings of dissatisfaction and discouragement. Focus on your own goals, progress, and achievements.

13. Practice patience: Building wealth and financial success are often gradual processes that require time and persistence. Be patient and prepared to face obstacles along the way. Keep focused on your long-term goals and do not let temporary setbacks demotivate you.

14. Take care of your financial and personal health: Remember that financial health is intrinsically linked to your personal health and well-being. Seek a healthy balance between work, finances, relationships, and self-care. Prioritize your physical and mental well-being, as this can have a positive impact on your ability to make sound financial decisions.

15. Share knowledge: As you gain experience and knowledge about finances, consider sharing your skills and teachings with others. This can be done through mentoring, contributing to online communities, or even sharing tips and advice with friends and family. By helping others achieve financial stability, you also reinforce your own knowledge and values.

Remember that the journey towards financial success is unique to each person and may require time, effort, and continuous adaptation. Be willing to adapt, learn from mistakes, and persevere towards your goals. With a disciplined approach, solid financial education, and a positive mindset, you are on the right path to achieving the success you desire.

To achieve success, it is important to develop the ability to handle large amounts of money and face the challenges that wealth and success bring. This requires discipline, determination, and a positive mindset.

Despite having lost everything, even ending up with not a single penny, these individuals managed to rebuild their fortunes. This is largely due to the mindset and skills they developed along the way. They have a deep understanding of how to handle money, invest wisely, make sound financial decisions, and seize opportunities as they arise.

These people have a mindset of resilience, persistence, and continuous learning. They understand that losses are part of the game and do not allow them to prevent them from seeking success again. Instead, they use their past experiences as valuable lessons and reasons to rise and start over.

Additionally, they know how to build and maintain solid relationships, both personal and professional. They understand the importance of surrounding themselves with trustworthy people, mentors, and business partners who can provide support, guidance, and opportunities.

Therefore, if you aspire to financial success, it is essential to awaken your inner energy, develop solid financial skills, and cultivate a mindset of growth and resilience. Remember that success is not just about accumulating wealth, but also about learning from challenges, growing as a person, and contributing positively to the world around you.

Be willing to learn from your experiences, persevere in the face of adversity, and seize opportunities as they arise. With determination, knowledge, and a positive mindset, you can build a solid foundation for financial success and achieve your goals. Remember that the journey is as important as the final destination, so enjoy every step along the way.

It is crucial to adopt a balanced approach to money. This means not only seeking financial prosperity but also valuing aspects such as health, relationships, emotional well-being, and contribution to society. True wealth goes beyond material possessions and involves finding a healthy balance in all areas of life.

Another important point is financial education. Constantly seek to learn about personal finance, investments, wealth management, and strategies to increase your income. Invest time and effort in enhancing your financial intelligence, whether through books, courses, mentors, or specialized consultants. The more you empower yourself in this area, the greater your ability to make informed financial decisions and achieve your goals.

Remember, financial success does not happen overnight. It is a continuous process that requires patience, discipline, and perseverance. Be prepared to face challenges along the way and be willing to adjust your strategy as needed.

Do not forget the importance of sharing your prosperity with others. As you achieve financial success, consider ways to give back to the community and make a difference in the lives of those around you. This not only brings great personal satisfaction but also contributes to a better and more balanced world.

Financial success is an individual and unique process for each person. Focus on awakening your inner energy, developing solid financial skills, seeking balance, and having a growth mindset. With dedication and perseverance, you are on the right path to achieving your financial goals and creating a life of sustainable prosperity.

Do not be afraid to dream big and work hard to achieve your goals. Over time, you will develop the ability to handle success and prosperity. Remember that success is a journey, not a destination. Keep learning, growing, and developing, and you will achieve everything you desire.

CHAPTER 21.

AWAKENING TO CONSCIOUSNESS: THE IMPORTANCE OF DEVELOPING OUR INNER ROOTS

Upon awakening to consciousness, we realize that most people act unconsciously, without understanding the impact of their actions. If we wish to change the results we are reaping, it is essential to modify the invisible roots that sustain these results.

Just like electricity, whose power we use and feel even without seeing it, there are intangible aspects in our lives that exert a direct influence on what manifests in the external world. If there are still doubts about this, just put your finger in the socket and feel the intensity of that energy.

As human beings, we are intrinsically interconnected with nature. By respecting its laws and tending to our inner world, our roots, life flows harmoniously. However, if we neglect these roots, we will face constant challenges to live fully. Awakening consciousness invites us to explore and understand these invisible roots that shape our experiences. It is through this awakening that we become aware of the impact of our choices, thoughts, and emotions on the world around us.

By recognizing these invisible roots, we gain the power to transform our lives. We can examine the limiting beliefs that prevent us from reaching our full potential and replace them with empowering beliefs. We can become aware of the behavioral patterns that sabotage us and choose new ways to act and react.

As we connect with the natural laws that govern the universe, we find alignment and fluidity. We learn to listen to our instincts, honor our values, and act in harmony with the world around us.

We recognize the interdependence between us and nature and take responsibility for being good stewards of our planet.

Awakening to consciousness invites us to seek internal and external balance. As we tend to our inner world, nurturing our mind, body, and spirit, we reflect this care onto the external world. In this way, we create a cycle of well-being and harmony that spreads beyond ourselves.

Therefore, upon awakening to consciousness, infinite possibilities for growth, transformation, and contribution open up. Through this awakening, we can shape a more conscious, loving, and sustainable reality for ourselves and future generations. It is an invitation to live purposefully, connected to the whole, and make a difference in the world.

Just as in a forest, farm, or orchard, it is what is beneath the surface, in the roots, that generates what manifests in the form of fruits. Therefore, it is futile to focus exclusively on the already ripe fruits. It is necessary to direct our attention to the care and development of the roots so that we can reap positive and lasting results.

By directing our focus to the inner roots, we are recognizing the importance of cultivating qualities such as self-mastery, self-awareness, and personal growth. It is through this introspection that we can identify and transform negative thought patterns, limiting beliefs, and destructive behaviors.

Instead of seeking quick and superficial solutions to the challenges we face, it is essential to delve into the depths of our being, exploring our values, purposes, and aspirations. By nurturing these inner roots, we strengthen the foundation upon which we build our lives.

Just as a careful gardener dedicates time and attention to the roots of a plant, watering them, fertilizing them, and removing weeds, we also need to nurture our inner life. This involves practices such as meditation, self-reflection, inspiring reading, personal skill development, and seeking knowledge.

As we delve into this inner journey, we begin to experience positive changes in our lives. Discipline, goal clarity, and organization naturally become part of our growth process. Through self-mastery and constant pursuit of personal evolution, we become capable of positively influencing the world around us.

As we develop this deep connection with our inner roots, we also cultivate the ability to find meaning in our experiences. We do not limit ourselves to merely reacting to life events, but learn to respond consciously and intentionally. By becoming aware of our internal values and purposes, we can make decisions aligned with them, rather than being influenced by external circumstances. By nurturing our inner selves, we strengthen our authenticity and ability to live a meaningful and purposeful life.

Moreover, as we become aware of our internal values and purposes, we also recognize the values and purposes we share with other human beings. This allows us to see our interconnectedness and interdependence, inspiring us to cultivate empathy, compassion, and mutual respect.

Nurturing our inner roots is not just an individual journey but also a contribution to collective well-being. As each of us dedicates ourselves to this inner work, we create a more conscious, compassionate, and harmonious society.

It is essential to dedicate time and attention to nurturing our inner roots. This empowers us to live authentically, meaningfully, and in harmony with ourselves and the world around us. It is a continuous journey of growth, transformation, and contribution that leads us to a fulfilling and realized life.

Therefore, as we look at the invisible roots that sustain our existence, we recognize that real transformation occurs from the inside out. By caring for and nurturing our roots, we are able to bear abundant fruits, achieve sustainable success, and live a meaningful and fulfilling life.

CHAPTER 22.

THE LAW OF CAUSE AND EFFECT: TRANSFORMING THE INTERIOR TO SHAPE THE EXTERIOR

We live in a world governed by the law of cause and effect. The true way to bring about change in our outer world is to modify our inner world. Whatever the panorama of outcomes in your life - whether abundance or scarcity, positive or negative - always remember that the world you see around you is just a reflection of what is happening within you. If things are not going well externally, it is a sign that something needs to be adjusted internally.

Everything that exists is composed of a single substance: energy. This energy travels and manifests itself in different frequencies and vibrations. Therefore, it is essential to understand that our thoughts, emotions, and beliefs emit an energetic frequency that attracts corresponding experiences in our external reality.

Although we may resist admitting it, there is a great deal of truth in the old proverb: "The apple doesn't fall far from the tree." When it comes to financial matters, we tend to replicate similar patterns to those of our parents - whether from one of them specifically or from a combination of both.

Even if you possess all the knowledge and qualifications in the world, if your mental model is not programmed for success, you are bound to face financial difficulties. Our beliefs and thought patterns about money, prosperity, and deservingness play a crucial role in our financial experiences.

Therefore, it is crucial to examine our ingrained beliefs regarding money, identify any blocks or limiting patterns, and reprogram our mental model for financial success. This involves cultivating an abundance mindset, adopting healthy financial habits, and seeking continuous personal growth.

By internally transforming our relationship with money and adopting a prosperous mindset, we open the doors to a new financial reality. Remember that you have the power to create your own financial story and break the cycle of repeating negative patterns from the past. By consciously choosing to think positively, cultivate gratitude, and act with intention, you are reprogramming your mind and attracting opportunities and abundance into your life.

However, inner transformation is not limited to the financial aspect alone. It encompasses all areas of our lives, such as relationships, health, career, and overall well-being. By working on our inner world, we are strengthening our foundation and creating the groundwork for our personal growth.

This requires a commitment to oneself, self-awareness, and self-discipline. It is necessary to examine our thoughts, emotions, and behaviors, identifying which are constructive and which need to be modified. As we become more self-aware, we can make choices more aligned with our values and goals.

To assist in this process, we can turn to practices such as meditation, visualization, positive affirmations, and self-care. Additionally, seeking knowledge, learning from mentors, and surrounding ourselves with positive and inspiring people can boost our personal growth.

Remember that inner transformation is an ongoing process. As we evolve and learn more about ourselves, we can adjust our perspectives and goals. Be patient with yourself, celebrate progress, and learn from challenges along the way.

By modifying your inner world, you are creating the conditions for a fuller, more meaningful, and abundant life. Remember that you have the power to shape your reality through the choices you make and the vibrations you emit. Start the transformation from within and observe the positive changes that will reflect in your outer world.

If you're dedicating yourself to saving money for tough times, think about what you'll really achieve. More tough days? It's time to rethink that approach. Instead of focusing on hoarding resources for bad times, direct your attention to building a financial reserve that will provide you with happy days and eventually achieve the coveted financial freedom. Believe in the law of attraction, for that is exactly what you will obtain.

Many people born into humble families feel anger and rebel against this situation. They generally strive and seek to become rich or, at the very least, have a strong impulse to do so. However, there is a significant problem, a real challenge to overcome. Even if these people amass fortunes or strive to achieve success, they often do not find happiness. Why? Because the roots of their wealth or motivation to make money are grounded in anger and resentment. Consequently, money and anger become associated entities in their minds: the more money they have or strive to obtain, the more their anger increases.

It's time to unravel this negative pattern and transform your approach. Seek harmony between prosperity and emotional well-being. Cultivate a positive mindset towards money, setting financial goals aligned with your values and aspirations. Remember that true wealth includes not only the material aspect but also inner peace and personal satisfaction. By unlinking money and anger, you will make room for a full and prosperous life, where happiness is the natural result of your financial achievements.

In the book of Proverbs, we find several examples that highlight the importance of a positive and balanced mindset regarding money. For example, in Proverbs 14:30, it is written: "A heart at peace gives life to the body, but envy rots the bones." This passage reminds us that inner peace and peace of mind are essential to enjoying a full life, regardless of financial circumstances.

Another example is found in 1 Timothy 6:10, which says: "For the love of money is a root of all kinds of evil. Some people, eager for money, have wandered from the faith and pierced themselves with many griefs." This passage warns us about the dangers of placing the love of money above all else, as it can lead to spiritual corruption and emotional suffering.

Furthermore, Jesus often spoke about the importance of not excessively worrying about material wealth. In Matthew 6:24, He says: "No one can serve two masters. Either you will hate the one and love the other, or you will be devoted to the one and despise the other. You cannot serve both God and money." This passage reminds us that our priority should be to seek a spiritual connection and dedicate ourselves to what is truly important, rather than being enslaved by the obsessive pursuit of wealth.

These biblical examples teach us the importance of a balanced approach to money, valuing inner peace, not prioritizing the love of money above all else, and seeking a life of purpose and spiritual connection. These principles help us find true happiness and fulfillment in all areas of our lives, including financial.

Take a deep reflection on your motivation to seek prosperity. Is it driven by a genuine desire to improve your life and the lives of others, or is it rooted in fear, anger, or the need for validation? By aligning your financial goals with your values and aspirations, cultivating a positive mindset, and seeking inner peace, you can create a life of abundance and fulfillment, where happiness is the natural result of your financial achievements.

"Make choices that make you feel rich and deserving. Once again, it is important to emphasize that the vibrational energy you emanate in these experiences will send the message to the universe that abundance is present in your life. And the universe, in response, will do its job, opening opportunities for you to receive even more.

While life is not a bed of roses and business demands dedication, it is essential to first ensure your livelihood. However, remember to reserve time to enjoy life. I never gave up my intention to achieve my two goals: financial prosperity and personal satisfaction. I never stayed for long in a job or business that I did not enjoy. In the end, I discovered that it was possible to become wealthy by doing what I loved.

Now, aware of this possibility, I continue to seek only jobs and projects that bring me pleasure. I understood that when we follow our passions and dedicate ourselves to what makes us happy, financial success becomes a natural consequence. I believe that each of us has the power to create an abundant reality, as long as we are aligned with our purposes and enjoy the path we walk.

Therefore, I encourage you to pursue your dreams, believe in your ability to achieve prosperity, and not give up on your passion. Remember that wealth is not limited only to the financial aspect but also to personal fulfillment and the happiness we find in our work. With persistence and determination, you can create a life of abundance in all aspects. Trust yourself and the power of the universe to conspire in your favor."

As you allow yourself to live a life of authentic wealth, recognizing your worthiness and flowing with what brings you joy, you are opening the doors to a journey of prosperity both material and spiritual.

So, forge ahead, navigate challenges with resilience, stand firm in your pursuit of jobs and projects that fill you with satisfaction and gratitude. Trust that the universe is responding to your deepest desires and wishes, bringing with it a steady flow of opportunities, abundance, and growth.

You are a potential co-creator, capable of manifesting a reality of fulfillment and success. Allow yourself to connect with the unlimited power of the universe and embark on this journey towards true enrichment, both in material terms and personal achievements.

Remember always: the universe is conspiring in your favor. Trust, believe, and open yourself to receive all that is rightfully yours. You deserve an abundant and prosperous life. Go ahead and create the reality you have always dreamed of. The universe is waiting to manifest through you."

Before managing a great fortune, it is essential to acquire the habit of being a creature of healthy financial habits. Therefore, the habit of managing money is more important than the amount you possess.

To start, it is crucial to control your expenses. Be aware of where your money is going and make a solid financial plan. An effective practice is to open a bank account dedicated to your personal finances. From this, regularly deposit 10% or more of your earnings into this account. Over time, look to invest this money to acquire assets that generate passive income streams.

The idea behind this strategy is to create a constant source of income that does not directly depend on your work. Just as the story of the richest man in Babylon teaches us, it is important to multiply our resources and make money work for us.

Therefore, building wealth is not just a matter of how much money you earn but of how you manage it and make it grow. By following solid principles such as investing wisely, saving regularly, and acquiring financial knowledge, we can pave the way to financial independence and truly become prosperous. With wisdom and discipline, you will be building a solid foundation for growth and success.

Remember that wealth is not only about the amount of money you possess but also about how you manage it and make it grow. Develop good financial habits, invest wisely, and cultivate a prosperous mindset. By following these principles, you will be setting yourself on the path to financial success and creating a life of abundance.

It is important to shift our focus from "active" income to "passive" income. Our thoughts influence our feelings, which in turn affect our actions, which lead to the results we seek. Success is not something innate but something that can be learned. We can acquire skills to win in any area. If you want to become an excellent golfer, you have the ability to learn and develop that skill. If music is your passion and you aspire to be a talented pianist, it is also possible to learn and improve in that field. True happiness can also be learned and achieved. Likewise, if you want to thrive financially, it is possible to learn the necessary strategies for that. Regardless of where you are currently, the most important thing is to be willing to learn and grow.

There is a saying that goes, "If you think education is expensive, try ignorance." This highlights the importance of knowledge, which is power. Power, in turn, is the ability to act effectively. Getting rich is not just about financial wealth. It also involves developing your character and mindset to achieve that goal. It is about who you become along this process, both in terms of character and mentally.

To achieve true enrichment, it is necessary to consider not only the financial aspect but also personal growth and character development. The journey towards success involves not only accumulating material wealth but also developing a positive mindset, work ethic, resilience, and leadership skills.

It is important to remember that success is a continuous process of learning. As we acquire knowledge and improve ourselves, we expand our ability to face challenges and seize opportunities. However, it is crucial to bear in mind that success does not happen overnight. It requires time, dedication, and perseverance.

No matter where you are right now, the essential thing is to be willing to learn, grow, and adapt. Education and self-development are valuable investments that yield results throughout life. By acquiring knowledge and skills, you empower yourself to make more informed decisions, identify opportunities, and overcome obstacles effectively.

Remember that true enrichment is not limited to material possessions but also encompasses personal fulfillment, emotional balance, and meaningful connections with others. As you strive to become the best version of yourself, you will not only achieve success but also enjoy a fulfilling and rewarding life.

Your subconscious mind is the fundamental principle that operates according to the law of faith. It is crucial to understand the meaning, function, and effectiveness of faith. The Bible expresses this in a simple, clear, and beautiful way: "Truly I tell you, if anyone says to this mountain, 'Go, throw yourself into the sea,' and does not doubt in their heart but believes that what they say will happen, it will be done for them." (Mark 11:23)

The law that governs your mind is the law of faith. This means having confidence in how your mind operates and believing in your own faith. Your mind's faith is simply the thought that dwells within it, nothing more and nothing less.

The response you receive from your subconscious mind corresponds to the nature of your thoughts. Therefore, it is essential to occupy your mind with concepts of harmony, health, peace, and goodwill. By doing so, true miracles can manifest in your life.

It is important to emphasize that the vast majority of humanity lives in the inner world. The most enlightened individuals are deeply interested in the inner world and recognize its importance. Understanding and mastering the underlying mind is the path to conquering a full and meaningful life.

Therefore, the wisest and most enlightened individuals dedicate time and effort to cultivate a positive and focused mind. They employ techniques such as creative visualization, affirmations, and meditation to nurture a mindset of success, abundance, and well-being.

By tuning into the inner world and cultivating elevated thoughts and mental states, they open themselves to a continuous flow of inspiration, intuition, and opportunities. These people understand that true transformation begins within themselves, and that it is from this internal place of power that they can create an extraordinary life.

So, stimulate your mind with positive thoughts and concepts, and you will see how your external reality will begin to align with your higher vision. By adopting this conscious and intentional approach, you will become the master of your inner world and experience the manifestation of true wonders in your life.

Most people in the world predominantly live in the realm of the inner world, where thoughts, feelings, and fantasies play a fundamental role. The most enlightened individuals have a great interest in the inner world. It is important to remember that it is the inner world that shapes your outer world. All the elements you encounter in your reality have been created by you, consciously or unconsciously, in the inner world of your mind.

Your subconscious mind is highly sensitive to your thoughts. They function as a mold or matrix through which flow the infinite intelligence, wisdom, vital forces, and energies of your subconscious.

The subconscious mind responds to the orders you give it based on what your conscious mind believes and accepts as truth. Therefore, it is crucial to be aware of the thoughts and beliefs you hold, as they have a powerful impact on creating your reality. By cultivating positive, empowering, and truthful thoughts, you establish a continuous flow of instructions to your subconscious, triggering a manifestation aligned with your intentions and deepest desires.

Your thoughts are like seeds planted in the fertile soil of your subconscious. As you feed your mind with positive, affirmative, and constructive thoughts, you are watering these seeds and allowing them to grow and flourish. On the other hand, if you focus on negative, self-deprecating, and limiting thoughts, you are nurturing seeds that produce undesirable results.

To create the reality you desire, it is essential that your conscious mind is aligned with your goals and aspirations. This means examining your beliefs, identifying and releasing negative thought patterns, and replacing them with positive thoughts that are in harmony with what you wish to manifest.

By doing so, you will be sending powerful instructions to your subconscious, activating its ability to attract the circumstances, opportunities, and resources necessary for the achievement of your goals. The subconscious makes no distinction between external reality and inner world; it simply responds to the orders given to it.

So, take control of your thoughts, strengthen your conscious mind, and nurture your inner world with positive and constructive thoughts. By doing so, you will become a conscious co-creator of your reality, using the power of your subconscious to manifest a life that is full, prosperous, and satisfying.

When you constantly affirm to others that you are incapable of something, your subconscious takes these affirmations literally and works to prevent you from achieving your desires. If you continue to say things like "I can't have that car," "I can't take that trip to Europe," "I can't have that house, that fur coat, or that mink stole," then your subconscious will follow your orders.

It is important to be careful with your thoughts and focus on everything that is true, honorable, fair, pure, lovely, and of good repute. Think about things that are virtuous and worthy of praise, as mentioned in Philippians 4:8.

True wealth is within you. Look inside yourself for the answers your heart seeks. The great secret of successful individuals throughout history has been their ability to connect with the subconscious and unleash the powers it contains.

When you learn to tap into your subconscious mind, you unlock unlimited potential. The great men and women of all ages understood this truth and used it to achieve great feats.

By connecting with your subconscious mind, you activate an endless source of creativity, intuition, and wisdom. It is capable of influencing your beliefs, thoughts, and behaviors, thus shaping your external reality.

To access the powers of your subconscious, it is important to cultivate a positive and affirmative mindset. Instead of focusing on what you cannot do, direct your attention to what is possible and achievable. Feed your mind with positive affirmations and vivid visualizations of your goals being accomplished.

The more you strengthen this connection with your subconscious, the more you will notice that it works in your favor. You will begin to notice synchronicities and opportunities that lead you in the right direction. Believe in the power of your subconscious and trust it to guide you toward success and the fulfillment of your dreams.

Remember that you are the commander of your mind. Therefore, choose your words and thoughts carefully, as they have the power to shape your reality. Believe in yourself, be kind with your words, and focus on what is positive and constructive. Thus, you will empower your subconscious to work for your benefit and achieve extraordinary results in your life.

Faith is a powerful thought that resides in the subconscious mind. Believe in the power of your subconscious to bring healing, inspiration, strength, and prosperity to your life. This will happen according to your faith.

By changing your thoughts, you can change your destiny. Your subconscious never sleeps or rests. It is always in operation, processing the information you send to it.

Your thoughts are received by the neurons, the cells that make up the brain. We are shaped by what we think. The subconscious mind is endowed with infinite intelligence and unlimited wisdom. It is fueled by hidden energies and is known as the law of life. Everything you engrave in your subconscious mind, it will move heaven and earth to make it come true.

And remember the words in the book of Matthew 21:22: "And whatever you ask in prayer, believing, you will receive." Have faith in your prayers and trust that they will be answered.

By understanding and using the power of your subconscious mind, you can transform your life in extraordinary ways. Believe in yourself, align your thoughts with your desires, and trust the process. Be the master of your subconscious mind and pave the way for the manifestation of your dreams and deepest aspirations.

You possess incredible power within you, capable of creating the reality you desire. Believe in the strength of your subconscious mind to overcome challenges, achieve healing, find inspiration, and thrive in all areas of your life.

Remember that your subconscious never rests. It is always in operation, absorbing and processing your thoughts, beliefs, and emotions. Therefore, it is essential to feed it with positive thoughts, powerful affirmations, and vivid visualizations of your goals being achieved.

You are the architect of your destiny, and every thought you engrave in your subconscious mind is like a seed that will be cultivated and manifested in your reality. Therefore, choose your thoughts carefully, as they have the power to shape your future.

The subconscious mind is a source of limitless wisdom. It has a connection to hidden energies and an intelligence that goes beyond conscious understanding. Trust in this higher intelligence and allow yourself to be guided by it.

When you pray or make requests to the universe, do so with faith and confidence. Believe that what you ask for will be received and manifested in your life. Keep in mind the words in the book of Matthew 21:22 and let that belief strengthen your faith.

Remember that you are the master of your mind. Take control of your thoughts, replace negative patterns with positive ones, and stay focused on what is desired. As you strengthen your connection with your subconscious and live according to your faith, you will pave the way for the fulfillment of your dreams and the creation of an extraordinary life.

THE END...